WOMEN'S STUDIES

edited by
Kathleen O'Connor Blumhagen
and
Walter D. Johnson

WOMEN'S STUDIES

CONTRIBUTIONS IN WOMEN'S STUDIES, NUMBER 2

An Interdisciplinary Collection

GP

GREENWOOD PRESS
WESTPORT, CONNECTICUT • LONDON, ENGLAND

Library of Congress Cataloging in Publication Data
Main entry under title:

Women's studies.

(Contributions in women's studies ; no. 2 ISSN 0147-104X)
Rev. presentations originally delivered at the 1976 meetings of the Western Social Science Association.
Bibliography: p.
Includes index.
1. Women's studies—United States—Addresses, essays, lectures. 2. Feminism—United States—Addresses, essays, lectures. I. Blumhagen, Kathleen O'Connor. II. Johnson, Walter D. III. Western Social Science Association. IV. Series.
HQ1181.U5W655   301.41'2'0973   77-18110
ISBN 0-313-20028-9

Library of Congress Catalog Card Number: 77-18110
ISBN: 0-313-20028-9
ISSN: 0147-104X

First published in 1978

Greenwood Press, Inc.
51 Riverside Avenue, Westport, Connecticut 06880

Printed in the United States of America

10 9 8 7 6 5 4 3 2 1

Contents

Preface

This volume owes much to the initial efforts of Charlotte Wolf of Ohio Wesleyan University. In 1974 Dr. Wolf, as a member of the Western Social Science Association's Executive Council, introduced the concept of Women's Studies as a topical area meriting recognition from the academy. With the backing of the council, Dr. Wolf requested that Rita Braito of the University of Denver initiate plans for the addition of a Women's Studies section to the association's 1975 annual meetings. Dr. Braito was joined by Shirley Nuss, then of the University of Colorado at Boulder and now of Wayne State University, and Kathleen O'Connor Blumhagen, then of Colorado Women's College and now of Pacific Lutheran University, who helped to develop the Women's Studies program. Although the initial results were limited in scope, due mainly to the time constraints, the interest generated clearly demonstrated the academic relevance of Women's Studies. Dr. Blumhagen was chosen to chair the Women's Studies section for the 1976 meetings.

After 1975 it became increasingly evident that the commitment to Women's Studies, both individually and institutionally, was even greater than had been anticipated. In addition to the participation of recognized leaders in the field, the section meetings attracted scholars whose identification with Women's Studies had previously been limited by the necessity of academic affiliation with established disciplines. It was also readily apparent that interest in Women's Studies was not limited to women scholars alone. Although in the minority, many of the participants were male.

The interest and concern elicited by these meetings, coupled with the unprecedented assemblage of professionals from throughout the social sciences to discuss issues emanating from Women's Studies, presented a unique opportunity. Recognizing this, the editors began to collect formal revised copies of the various presentations at the 1976 meetings for review and potential publication. The essays contained herein are the results of that process.

While there were many excellent papers to chose from, it was our concerted opinion that the selections contained in this edition best represented the history, direction, and issues surrounding the advent of Women's Studies. While we owe much to our many colleagues who helped us in the preparation of this manuscript, the final decisions and therefore the responsibility for its contents are ours.

We are deeply indebted to the Western Social Science Association for providing the vehicle by which this work became a reality. Particularly noteworthy was the time and effort given by Dr. Sidney Heitman, Editor of the *Social Science Journal*, and his staff in preparing the original version of this publication and sponsoring it for book publication. Our special thanks go to Nancy Nichols of Sangamon State University's library staff, who prepared much of the bibliographical guide, and to Jeff Radcliffe, also of Sangamon State University, whose long hours spent in library research and detail verification were of immense help. Also, the typing and editing skills of Jan Matta and Libby King have been invaluable.

Most of all, however, we would like to express our gratitude and support to those who have worked and continue to work for the establishment and recognition of Women's Studies as a necessary and vibrant addition to our educational system.

August 1977   Kathleen O'Connor Blumhagen
                                            Pacific Lutheran University
                                            Tacoma, Washington

                                            Walter D. Johnson
                                            Sangamon State University
                                            Springfield, Illinois

Introduction

Although Women's Studies occupies a relatively youthful position within the academic arena, its roots are very deep. Women's Studies, as pointed out by Sarah Slavin Schramm in the opening essay, is a parallel event to the resurgence of the Women's Movement that occurred in the mid-1960s. It represents a realization that the principles upon which the movement flourished rest on a strong intellectual base and that the need for knowledge about women and for women has a legitimate place within academia. Women's Studies is a vehicle for change and expression and is an integral part of the larger context of the feminist movement. As such, it is not static, nor is it designed to be so.

In addition to the issue of dynamics, and in spite of the rapid increase in programs in recent years, Women's Studies continues to be confronted with the question of effectiveness. Sarah Hoagland, in "The Reeducation of Sophie," argues that the framework within which a Women's Studies program must exist is crucial. Two elements are determinative in this respect: the type of program selected and the attitude that exists toward the female student. Dr. Hoagland contends that only through the adoption of a multidisciplinary approach in the context of a coeducational setting can the traditional conditioned attitudes toward women be overcome. In addition to what form Women's Studies should take, there exists the question of content. Operating in an already established program, much like that envisaged by Dr. Hoagland, Ellen Boneparth examines the need for continued evaluation. While agreeing with the interdisciplinary nature of Women's Studies, Dr. Boneparth notes that only through an ongoing assessment of its components can Women's Studies programs maintain their relevance and effectiveness.

Throughout these essays there runs an undercurrent of agreement that Women's Studies must actively seek to expand its body of knowledge, partly by challenging the assumptions of traditional research. While numerous examples come to mind, two essays have been chosen for inclusion because they so aptly demonstrate the effects of male-dominated priorities in research. As Drs. Mary Stewart and Pat Erickson point out in their article, "The Sociology of Birth," pregnancy, labor, and birth are experiences that are traditionally viewed as an integral part of being a woman. Since it is an experience that is specifically female, it has not in the past occasioned the interest of many social scientists. Even the medical sciences have devoted precious little time and effort to researching the broader area of women's health in comparison to men's. A similar situation was found by Joyce Griffen in her examination of cross-cultural material available concerning "Behavior Changes at Menopause." The masculine dominance of research orientation may go beyond the choice of topics, however. Dr. Griffen raises the question of whether even when women do examine topics specific to them, they are not so acculturated by their backgrounds and their training, so caught up in the objectivist approach, that they, too, lose their feminist perspective.

The articles by Jane Slaughter and Sylvia Gonzales are further reminders that the current feminist movement is neither new nor complete. Dr. Slaughter's work details the activities of several women, particularly Angelica Balabanoff, in the socialist movement of the early part of this century. Their lives and their attraction to the issue of Women's Rights closely parallel that of their modern-day contemporaries. Although they adhered to the socialist goal of equality of humankind, these women were keenly aware of the relationship of its attainment to their own emancipation. For them, socialism provided the organization, the vehicle, for translating their idea of power into action. Today, a similar situation exists with minority women. Their battle against discrimination and oppression, vividly portrayed in the article by Dr. Gonzales, must be waged on two fronts: one racial and the other sexual. Realization of their goals in one area does not necessarily diminish the scope of their problems in the other. Thus, while the feminist movement holds some promise for Chicanas, its success depends to a large degree on its compatibility with the objectives of racial and cultural equality for Chicano people as a whole.

The last three articles provide examples of research designed specifically to expand the core of knowledge on issues related directly to women. Thomas M. Uhlman and Herbert M. Kritzer examine the hypothesis that because women undergo a different socialization process in our culture, their decision-making behavior will also differ. This has often been used as a discriminatory tactic in denying positions of authority to women. Utilizing the office of trial judgeships in a large metropolitan city as their testing ground, Drs. Kritzer and Uhlman found no indication of sex-differentiated behavior to substantiate this hypothesis. In a similar vein, Laura Katz Olson's study of sex-linked values in engineering serves to dispel the myths surrounding the issue of why so few women enter this profession. The tendency, again, has been to focus on the social, political, and psychological predispositions of women. While not arguing against the existence of differences in values and interests between men and women, Dr. Olson's in-depth interviews with college students suggest other factors are at play. She concludes that economic, institutional, and structural barriers are far more accountable for the paucity of women in engineering and that until policies are adopted to correct these problems, the situation is likely to continue. The last article, by Susan A. MacManus and Nikki R. Van Hightower, examines the impact of local government tax structures on women. Based on the data presented in their study, Drs. MacManus and Van Hightower conclude that local tax structures are biased against women, particularly those who are single or heads of households. Thus, like many other policies, local government tax structures, rather than helping to alleviate economic imbalances, serve to further aggravate them.

Though furthering the state of the art, these articles serve to indicate that much remains to be done in the area of Women's Studies. Research must continue. Educational programs must be supported. Women must continue to translate their needs into action. It is hoped that this volume will assist in this endeavor. Like the Women's Movement in general, this collection is not the first effort, nor can it be the last.

WOMEN'S STUDIES

SARAH SLAVIN SCHRAMM
George Washington University

Women's Studies: Its Focus, Idea Power, and Promise[1]

The growth and increasing stability of Women's Studies continue to both amaze and dismay many observers. Nevertheless, that growth is well documented, and the stability is well earned. An analysis, at this point in the development of Women's Studies, of its focus, idea power, and promise, seems appropriate.

WOMEN'S STUDIES: FOCUS

We were teaching about women before we had a name for it.[2]

The resurgence of the women's movement with the establishment of federal and state Commissions on the Status of Women, the issuance of Betty Friedan's *The Feminine Mystique,* and the insertion of the class "sex" to Title VII of the 1964 Civil Rights Act all had a definite intellectual component. The works of Shulamith Firestone, Kate Millett, Alice Rossi, and Naomi Weisstein exhibit this. The intellectual component extended far beyond the works of a few individuals, however.

In 1968, the Women's History Research Center at Berkeley was collecting and publicizing material by and about women. In 1969, nineteen members of National Organization for Women (NOW) came together to found Know, Inc., a publishing house directed toward the dissemination of serious feminist writing. By the end of 1970, the Modern Language Association's Commission on the Status of Women listed 110 college and university courses dealing with women. The following year witnessed a sixfold proliferation of formal, largely introductory, and interdisciplinary courses about women and the availability of at least seventeen formal programs. Today, five years later (1976 — Ed.), according to the latest listing in *Women's Studies Newsletter,* there are 151 such programs.[3] Departmental offerings, especially in English, Sociology, and History, are continually surfacing. High school and professional/vocational schools are also beginning to include courses in their curriculums.

Florence Howe and Carol Ohmann noted the geographic coincidence of the Women's Movement per se and Women's Studies in volume 3 of the *Female Studies* series.[4] Early in 1973, in recognition of the congruence of Women's Studies and the goals of the National Organization for Women, Anne Grant and this writer established a national Committee to Promote Women's Studies. Originally an appendage to NOW's Education Task Force, the Committee soon achieved independent status. Women's Studies and the Women's Movement were united.

Simultaneously, consciousness-raising emerged as a small scale organizational mechanism with broad implications for the Women's Movement.[5] The rap group had been part of the experience of women activists disillusioned by the sexism of the civil rights and peace movements. Ultimately it was to reach into the homes of countless "uninvolved" women in every part of the country. Its impact was being felt in Women's Studies settings as well. Gerda Lerner noted in volume 2 of the *Female Studies* series that students in her seminar at Sarah Lawrence were revealing "deep-seated doubts and problems . . . concerning their own roles as women in society."[6] By the time *Female Studies* 7 was published three years later, Deborah Silverton Rosenfelt cited "self-actualization and consciousness-raising" as traditional Women's Studies components.[7]

Developmentally, neither the intellectual nor the affective dimension of Women's Studies has been solely confined to the university. They have flourished in continuing education settings, in storefronts and women's centers, in preschools and community programs, and in a variety of alternative forms of education. Furthermore, Women's Studiers working from within formal programs often developed ties with the community.[8] Even with this environmental diversity, the focus of Women's Studies has been remarkably unitary. It includes: (1) increasing the visibility of women's accomplishments; (2) dispersing information and resources on women which ordinarily are bypassed; (3) defining feminism for the community; (4) contributing to the legitimacy of a movement which aims for nothing less than human liberation; (5) facilitating consciousness-expansion in others; and (6) increasing the levels of consciousness of Women's Studiers themselves.[9]

Of the items which make up this focus, one and two may seem relatively intellectual in scope and five and six relatively affective, with three and four combining both dimensions. This impression is somewhat deceptive. Delving into the resources which contain, for example, women's history and uncover women's contributions to all facets of life constitute consciousness-raising experiences in themselves. Affective encounters, on the other hand, seldom are conducted apart from intellectual perceptions linking them to the past and to thought about the future. Attempts to explicate feminism and to support the Women's Movement rely on both dimensions and reflect the interaction between them.

These interactive dimensions, appearing as they did in widely diverse environments, essentially had three implications. The first implication was a personal one, reaching nearly all of those who engaged in Women's Studies. These individuals, whatever their backgrounds, exhibited increased levels of assertive behavior and wholehearted application of themselves to realizing their potentials. This phenomenon has been commented on extensively throughout the *Female Studies* series. In addition, Kathleen O'Connor Blumhagen has shown statistically significant change in ego levels of student women enrolled in a Women's Studies course over the length of one semester.[10]

The two remaining implications extend to the university and to the Women's Movement itself and have not been explored widely or systematically. These implications were the product of an idea power which grew to activist proportions with the diverse manifestations of the intellectual and affective dimensions. It is to the idea power of Women's Studies that this analysis now turns.

WOMEN'S STUDIES: IDEA POWER

What I want back is what I was
Before the bed, before the knife,
Before the brooch-pin and the salve
Fixed me in this parenthesis;
Horses fluent in the wind,
A place, a time gone out of mind.[11]

With increasing self-awareness among Women's Studiers and more hard data at their disposal, they gradually learned that traditional ivory tower structures and procedures for disseminating scholarship were not amenable to a radical change of perspective on women's roles. Universities, after all, generally are hierarchical in structure and conflict-oriented in procedure. Centering on personalities and coalitions, a conflict-orientation is one in which there is continuous strife for mastery. Hostile encounters are frequent, prolonged, and to be expected, as are competition and polemics.[12] The universities, which set the tone for all of educationdom, were not ready for a raised consciousness about women.[13]

Unlike oil and water, sexism and scholarship apparently do mix. Despite Mary Beard's assertion that women are a force in history with which to contend,[14] Simone de Beauvoir found it necessary to point out that all of women's history is man-made, a sort of Caucasian masculine burden.[15] Discipline after discipline was found wanting as numerous women scholars, and some men, compiled statistics and conducted content analyses of the representation of women in person as faculty or in substance as data. Victoria Schuck and Judy Corder Tully, in a symposium issue of *Social Science Quarterly,* conceptualized these lapses as "masculine blinders."[16]

It remained for Women's Studies, like Black Studies and the Free School movement before it, to undertake an overt adjustment of the emphases being placed on white male accomplishments and history by the academy. The exclusionary nature of the academy in this regard was exposed by the operations of Women's Studiers within and without academia. Such exposure at times led to a forceful backlash against women who committed themselves without reserve to the new discipline.[17] The collective structure and procedure of Women's Studies had confronted an entrenched historical system which systematically excluded women and minorities. That Women's Studies confronted it and survived was an accomplishment in itself. That it also was able to grow and even to flourish under such conditions is a genuine tribute to its idea power.

The important point lies with the growing recognition of the inconsistency between the academy's conflict-orientation and Women's Studies' more collective nature. Centering on issues and consensus, a collective orientation is one which takes into consideration individuals as well as the group.[18] Mary Daly sees the prime ethic as one of attraction.[19] Marilyn Salzman-Webb discussed this aspect of Women's Studies relatively early.[20] At times the recognition of it was overt enough to stimulate a university-affiliated Women's Studies program to seek an autonomous locale within that university. This was the case with the Women's Studies College at the State University of New York/Buffalo. The inconsistency was apparent, and most if not all Women's Studiers in a university setting had to deal with it.

As time went on, Women's Studiers were verbalizing feminist assumptions in a consistent and coherent fashion.[21] These assumptions included: (1) the presence of a historically valid women's culture which is knowable and relevant to women's lives today;[22] (2) the sisterhood of all women, across race, creed, religion, sexual preference, economic status, and national origin, grounded in a common oppression;[23] (3) the need to facilitate consciousness of this oppression among Women's Studiers, activists in the Women's Movement, and other women and to change that oppressed status;[24] and (4) the necessity of reaching prior consensus among these groups of individuals by means of a collective process about the means by which to seek change in that status.[25] The explication of these assumptions had an ideological implication for the Women's Movement that was wide-ranging and startling.

For those pragmatic activists who devoted themselves almost exclusively to a legal/legislative approach to change in women's status, with a corresponding commitment to traditional political tactics, the explication of feminist assumptions created a serious dilemma. Viewed on the basis of these assumptions, their tactics were inconsistent with them. Worse, their tactics were identifiably the same conflict-oriented tactics utilized by the academy to the detriment of women and minorities.[26]

The basic inconsistency between feminist assumptions and activist tactics effectually retarded any impetus to develop overall organizational strategy. It also was detrimental to the development of Women's Movement ideology. Social movements of great scope generally have embraced great ideologies, but as Jo Freeman has observed, the Women's Movement experienced an almost total absence of coherent ideology.[27] As Women's Studies explicated feminist assumptions and moved closer to the Women's Movement rather than being subsumed within the academy, the possibility for grounding movement activism in such ideology grew much greater.[28]

Ideology offers an elaborate, closely woven, and far-ranging structure which is more abstract than either strategy or tactics. Strategy is formulated with a view toward the future, incorporating tactics which are designed to capture an immediate advantage. It is strategy which propounds the broad direction within which tactics are mustered. The problem for the activist is to utilize tactics which are not self-defeating in the long run. Consistency among ideology, strategy, and tactics affords the most efficient means for any social movement simultaneously to consolidate its gains and to project its program into the future.[29]

Without ideological, strategic, and tactical consistency, it is not likely that those who devote themselves to seeking comprehensive change in women's status will attain it. An established socioeconomic and political system which changes only by increments and which responds only to those with authorized access to it is not amenable to their efforts. In fact, such a system maintains itself through the activities of the actors within it relying on relative quietude among those not recruited to its top. The demands of those with access to the system's hierarchy are converted into policy. Access is not granted gratuitously. Ironically, those who support the system by their quietude do not necessarily gain access to it. They receive only the most minimal of rewards for their acquiescence.

Those who support the system but seek a greater share of its outputs may be shunned or punished for their deviance. If they are willing to forego their deviant behavior to return to their former quietude or if they show unusual ability to adapt to the rules of the game as it is being played, then they may not be punished. In some cases, their share of the distribution of values even may be increased, but it will not be increased wholesale. It will be increased either by granting them maximum *feasible* participation, which is likely to be diminished after a period of time, or an increment of some value, for example the issuance of regulations for Title IX legislation which are not likely to be implemented extensively.[30]

On the other hand, groups of individuals who are able to create a serious imbalance in the system's environment will set into motion a dynamic process of adjustment which ultimately can accommodate their demands. The exchange here leads to an equilibrium in the system once again, but in the meantime changes are made in the system's overall components and in their combination. The only other alternative for change seems to be outright revolution in the modern sense — that is, probably violent overthrow of the entire system. This does not seem to be a likely event, and chances are it would not be a desirable one.[31] Groups of individuals who achieve such an adjustment must be organized, self-disciplined, and internally consistent in their ideology, strategy, and tactics. Without such consistency, neither organization nor discipline is likely to be effective or long-lived.

The solution to the dilemma of inconsistency among ideology, strategy, and tactics, or inconsistency of the sort which inhibits development of one or more of them, lies with conscious attempts to create structures and procedures better suited to women's needs than those of a historical system which largely has denied them. Conscious attempts along these lines are typical of the idea power which characterizes Women's Studies. An example of such conscious attempts is the development within Women's Studies of collective structures and procedures subversive of institutions, disciplines, and processes of thought which in the past ignored matters of utmost concern to women. This is where idea power has its fullest impact. It is to the framework for these alternative structures and procedures that this analysis now turns.

WOMEN'S STUDIES: PROMISE

I refuse to allow you, Beadle though you are, to turn me off the grass. Lock up your libraries if you like; but there is no gate, no lock, no bolt that you can set upon the freedom of my mind. [32]

It is a conscious perspective of women's own which is required. It is the ability to translate the freedom of their minds into the minds of others, thereby awakening what Virginia Woolf called "the common life which is the real life."[33] This reality association, this realization of potentiality, is far from the "living AS IF . . ." of which Doris Lessing writes in *The Golden Notebook*.[34] And while Woolf sees the common life as the androgynous one, Women's Studiers, at this crossroad at least, are using feminist assumptions to frame the future at the same time they explore the here and now.[35] Only as ideas and actions, future and present, are fused, can women and men be capable of someday, some century, being born under an androgynous sign.

Woolf herself recognized the immense problems presented by attempts to change an entrenched historical system. She is adamant in her response to the problem, however. As one commentator has stated:

Beneath the institutional level, [she] perceived that the social system and its particular institution were maintained on the personal level, in part by the acquiescence and collaboration of those who accepted the system's values and chose to seek its rewards, and in part by the ruthless punishment, exclusion and even destruction of those who might seek to change it. . . . Woolf knew that this system would not be changed with the touch of a wand . . . . But she saw too that that system could not be overthrown by imitating it.[36]

The promise of Women's Studies as ideology and organizational strategy lies in its collective orientation, in effect a refusal to imitate the conflictual orientation of the prevailing system. This collective orientation is the result of Women's Studies' dual dimensionality, its focus on both the intellectual and the affective. The interaction and potential for integration of these two dimensions contributes to an emphasis on the group as a collection of individual women or, conversely, on individual women as members of a group. Intellectually, Women Studiers collectively tap and expand resources, internalizing knowledge and its personal implications. Affectively, they explore with significant others in ever-widening circles their awareness of oppressed status and the need to change that status.

What is especially important here is the ability to work collectively. Such a process is at least possible and practicable, given a reliance on assumptions about the relevance of women's culture, sisterhood, and its potential for facilitating change in women's status. It involves looking toward the future aggregate well-being of a diverse class, namely women. The attainment of consensus on how best to achieve such well-being, and why it is to be achieved at all, is contingent on women's overall diversity. It is achievable, however, only where there is agreement that women have some things in common with one another.[37] General agreement on these matters is the basis on which to organize in a disciplined and internally consistent fashion as activists seeking change in women's status.

The collective process is to a certain degree a conceptual mechanism in that it nowhere exists in pure form. It is not absolutely attainable.[38] It could be visualized as a goal, something to be attained so far as is possible as women transcend their Freudian-prescribed destiny. It must be emphasized, though, that it has been tested in Women's Studies settings and found fit. It is, however, no nirvana. Attempts to achieve it so far as is possible can and do sometimes result in failure. The widespread factionalism within the mid-1970's Women's Movement is evidence of such failure, just as it is evidence of the internalized inconsistency examined above.

The ability to utilize a collective process implies maturity in the group of individuals working to achieve it. It consists of the willingness to seek out critical combinations of diverse viewpoints on both the intellectual and affective levels. It thus combines knowledge about women generally, about women's status and potential, and about feminist assumptions with the awareness of what all this means to women personally. By gathering such knowledge and seeking such awareness in diverse environments, Women's Studiers have engaged in the beginnings of a collective process. Their ability to organize and to persevere, often in the midst of detractors, has been tested. This is the promise of Women's Studies as ideology and organizational strategy.

Such promise admittedly has its problems. To control Women's Studies from within is not an easy matter. There are various administrators, scholars, students, and Women's Studiers embodying particular political persuasions who seek such control. The interaction of intellectual and affective dimensions in Women's Studies continues to frighten and/or exasperate some individuals. Financial support is a necessary and troublesome aspect of the promotion of Women's Studies. The question of whether it is better to integrate more traditional disciplines or to strike out for separate status goes unanswered.

Still, Women's Studiers are not unfamiliar with the problem of control; it is at the heart of every change they seek. The supposed dichotomy of intellect and affect may in the end be a non-issue; as *Female Studies 6* points out, "The pain and invigoration of *being* personal is no longer a subject in itself."[39] Those who most fear "ghettoization" may in time come around to the conclusion that Women's Studies is worthy of separate status and can withstand critical scrutiny. Isolation and excision are by no means inevitable outcomes of such status, especially given the fact and potential of community ties.

It is the promise of Women's Studies that is pursued in the release of its idea power. Through Women's Studies, the broadest approach to sexism of all, one which inculcates feminist assumptions and institutional change, can be undertaken. The promise of Women's Studies as ideology and organizational strategy is wholly indigenous; it is a perspective of women's own.

NOTES

1. An earlier version of this article, "Women's Studies as Organizational Strategy," was delivered at the Western Social Science Association Meeting, Arizona State University, Tempe, April 30, 1976.

2. Elaine Showalter, "Introduction: Teaching about Women," *Female Studies 4*, ed. Elaine Showalter and Carol Ohmann, (Pittsburgh: Know, Inc., 1971), p. i.

3. *Women's Studies Newsletter* (Old Westbury, N.Y.), Winter 1976, pp. 8-11.

4. Showalter and Ohmann, pp. iv-v.

5. Richard E. Johnson, "The Future of Humanistic Psychology," *The Humanist*, vol. 35 (March/April 1975), pp. 5-7, describes the power of awareness. Juliet Mitchell, *Woman's Estate* (New York: Random House; Vintage Books, 1973), p. 178, outlines a potential problem.

6. Gerda Lerner, "The Many Worlds of Women," *Female Studies 2,* ed. Florence Howe (Pittsburgh: Know, Inc., 1970), p. 87.

7. Deborah Silverton Rosenfelt, "Introduction," *Female Studies 3* (Old Westbury, N.Y.: The Feminist Press, 1973), p. viii.

8. Catherine Stimpson, "Women's Studies and the Community: Some Models," *Women's Studies Newsletter* (Old Westbury, N.Y.), Summer 1974, pp. 2-3, discusses this relationship and its potential.

9. Sarah Slavin Schramm, "Do-It-Yourself: Women's Studies," *Female Studies 8*, ed. Sarah Slavin Schramm (Pittsburgh: Know, Inc., 1975), p. 3.

10. Kathleen O'Connor Blumhagen, "The Relationship Between Female Identity and Feminism" (unpublished Ph.D. dissertation, Washington University, 1974).

11. Sylvia Plath, *The Eye-Mote, The Colossus and Other Poems* (New York: Random House; Vintage Books, 1968), p. 13.

12. Marilyn Salzman-Webb, "Feminist Studies: Frill or Necessity," *Female Studies 5* (Pittsburgh: Know, Inc., 1972), pp. 64-76. Party politics and the U. S. government constitute other examples of this model. For instance, see James McGreagor Burns, *The Deadlock of Democracy: Four-Party Politics in America with a New Perspective for the 70s* (Englewood Cliffs, N.J.: Prentice-Hall, 1967).

13. Joan I. Roberts, *Creating a Facade of Change; Informal Mechanisms Used to Impede the Changing Status of Women in Academe* (Pittsburgh: Know, Inc., 1975).

14. Mary Beard, *Women As a Force in History; A Study in Traditions and Realities* (New York: Macmillan, 1946).

15. Simone de Beauvoir, *The Second Sex*, trans. H. M. Parshley (New York: Alfred Knopf, 1952), pp. 118-19; June Sochen, *Herstory: A Woman's View of American History* (New York: Alfred Publishing Co., 1974), pp. 3-4.

16. Victoria Schuck and Judy Corder Tully, "A Symposium: Masculine Blinders in the Social Sciences," *Social Science Quarterly*, vol. 55 (Dec. 1974), pp. 564-656.

17. Wisconsin, Department of Industry, Labor and Human Relations, Equal Rights Division, Initial Determination, Dr. Joan I. Roberts *vs.* John Weaver, President, University of Wisconsin/Madison, *et al.*, ERD Case #7400847, EEOC TMK #4-1200, is an example of such a case. Also "Fact Sheet: Joan Roberts *vs.* University of Wisconsin/Madison," in *The Newsheet: Notes from the NOW Committee to Promote Women's Studies* (Cherry Hill, N. J.), Nov. 1974; excerpted in *Off Our Backs* (Washington, D. C.), Dec. 1974, p. 3.

18. Joan Borod *et al.*, "Teaching Collectively," *Women's Studies Program; Three Years of Struggle* (San Diego: California State University), pp. 42-3.

19. Mary Daly, *Beyond God the Father; Toward a Philosophy of Women's Liberation* (Boston: Beacon Press, 1973), p. 198. A contemporary example here is the "think tank" Sagaris, for example, an independent institute for the study of feminist thought, where alternatives to existing structures and procedures are being created. A historical example would be the community concept of the quilting bee, an early manifestation of women's culture in this country as portrayed in Ruth Finley, *Old Patchwork Quilts and the Women Who Made Them* (New York: Branford, 1929).

20. Marilyn Salzman-Webb, pp. 64-5.

21. The author's forthcoming *Plow-Women Rather than Reapers; An Intellectual History of Feminism in the United States* (Metuchen, N.J.: Scarecrow Press, 1978) offers a historical treatment of the parameters of feminism.

22. Evelyn Reed, *Woman's Evolution; From Matriarchal Clan to Patriarchal Family* (New York: Pathfinder Press, 1975); Jane Alpert, "Forum: Mother Right—A New Feminist Theory," *Ms.*, vol. 2 (Aug. 1973), pp. 52-55; Elizabeth Gould Davis, *The First Sex* (New York: G. P. Putnam's Sons, 1971).

23. Robin Morgan, *Sisterhood Is Powerful:*

An Anthology of Writings from the Women's Liberation Movement (New York: Random House, 1970); "Forum: Rights of Passage," *Ms.*, vol. 4 (Sept. 1975), pp. 74-98. Deborah Rosenfelt, "What Happened at Sacramento," *Women's Studies Newsletter* (Old Westbury, N. Y.), Fall, 1973, p. 1, discusses this concept under fire.

24. Shulamith Firestone, *The Dialectic of Sex: The Case for Feminist Revolution* (New York: William Morrow and Co., 1970).

25. Marilyn Salzman-Webb, *News Bulletin* (Pittsburgh: Know, Inc., Sept. 1975), discusses the process in the context of the Know collective's own experiences. See also Deirdre English and Barbara Ehrenreich, "Women Writing Together," *The Feminist Press; News/Notes 4* (Old Westbury, N. Y.), 1973, p. 2. See Kate Millet, *Flying* (New York: Alfred A. Knopf, 1974), pp. 59-60, for a discussion of the process gone wrong and yet viable.

26. Warren T. Farrell, "Women's and Men's Liberation Groups: Political Power within the System and without the System," *Women in Politics*, ed. Jane S. Jaquette (New York: John Wiley, 1974), pp. 171-201; Marin L. Carden, *The New Feminist Movement* (New York: Russell Sage Foundation, 1974), pp. 166-71.

27. Jo Freeman, *The Politics of Women's Liberation* (New York: David McKay, 1976), p. 10.

28. That Women's Studies was not subsumed stems from the diverse environment within which it developed. Many important contributions to it have been entirely extra-academy.

29. Nancy Porter, with Julie Allen and Jean Maxwell, "The Future of Women's Studies: From Portland State University — In Three Voices," *Women's Studies Newsletter* (Old Westbury, N. Y.), Spring 1975, p. 5.

30. David Easton, *A Framework for Political Analysis* (Englewood Cliffs, N. J.: Prentice-Hall, 1965); David B. Truman, *The Governmental Process; Political Interests and Public Opinion* (2nd ed.; New York: Alfred A. Knopf, 1971).

31. Hannah Arendt points out that revolutions are not "mere changes." The once astronomic term in modern usage implies an irrevocable, irresistible movement gone out of control (*On Revolution* [New York: Viking Press, 1965], pp. 13-52). The radical experiment Shulamith Firestone proposes in her case for feminist "revolution" is not the uncontrolled momentum which Arendt traces. Experiment in and of itself implies controls. Firestone's program of simultaneously existing, interwoven multiple options cannot be achieved by revolution in the modern sense.

32. Virginia Woolf, *A Room of One's Own* (New York: Harcourt, Brace, and World, 1957), pp. 78-9.

33. *Ibid.*, p. 79.

34. Doris Lessing, *The Golden Notebook* (New York: Alfred A. Knopf, 1973), p. ix. (Lessing's emphasis.)

35. Nancy Topping Bazin, *Virginia Woolf and the Androgynous Vision* (New Brunswick, N. J.: Rutgers University Press, 1973).

36. Bernice A. Carroll, " 'To Crush Him in Our Own Country': The Political Thought of Virginia Woolf," paper delivered at the Third Berkshire Conference on Women's History, Bryn Mawr College, June 10, 1976; excerpts from pp. 29, 31.

37. Juliet Mitchell makes this point narrowly, confining it to the stage at which women become aware of their oppressed status, pp. 73-4. In doing so, she overlooks the interconnectedness of feminist assumptions.

38. Douglas W. Rae, "The Limits of Consensual Decision," *American Political Science Review*, vol. 69 (Dec. 1975), pp. 1270-94, and in the same issue, Gordon Tullock, "Comment on Rae's 'The Limits of Consensual Decision,'" pp. 1295-97.

39. Nancy Hoffman, Cynthia Secor and Adrian Tinsley (eds.), *Female Studies 6* (Old Westbury, N. Y.: The Feminist Press, 1972), p. 1.

SARAH HOAGLAND
Northeastern Illinois University—Chicago

On the Reeducation of Sophie

Many Women's Studies programs have sprung up across the country and more will follow. The job has begun in earnest. At times the mere goal of acquiring a few courses seemed unattainable, especially in light of the prevailing and persisting presumption that Women's Studies lacks academic substance. Besides breaking new ground, designing new classes, and bringing new perspectives to bear on traditional material as well as traditional approaches, Women's Studies faculties have been on the defensive. Programs must be justified and safeguarded, publishers persuaded to accept new material, and research defended to doubting colleagues. In addition, the weeding out of Women's Studies faculty for what is said to be inadequate progress in traditional areas must be resisted. Taken as a whole, the practical problems were, and still are, insurmountable. So many have jumped in, and although they have not resolved all the problems, they realize the issues involved are substantive.

Now that several programs have been established, however, important decisions must be made. Two areas necessitating such decisions are (1) the type of program which will likely succeed, and (2) the attitude adopted toward the female student. In order to give focus to the discussion of these issues, the traditional approach to the education of women, as enunciated by Jean Jacques Rousseau in *Emile*, will be introduced and examined. For not only did Rousseau discourage women's intellectual development, but he also encouraged female dependency.

One alternative, adopted in the past to foster this tradition and thought recently to combat it, has been the all-women's college. A second alternative to this traditional approach has been the institution of separate departments of Women's Studies. Both of these options are in turn examined and discussed. There is an attitude toward female students seemingly implicit in the first two alternatives which must be guarded against on pain of perpetuating the Rousseauian tradition and thus the academic and social status quo. What is feasible is the establishment of multidisciplinary or area studies programs.

THE TRADITION

Much of modern educational theory derives from the work of Jean Jacques Rousseau. One of the more unfortunate aspects of his theory addresses itself to the education of women and stems from the view that men are active and strong while women are passive and weak. From this, he argued, it follows that women are intended to be pleasing to men. He did not explain the logic of his argument, but apparently his reasoning was this: As a result of a bio-logical difference, men and women possess different characters. What are seen as defects in the male character are viewed as good qualities in women. Hence a woman is cunning, a quality she possesses in compensation for her lesser strength. This allows her to control men while remaining loyal and obedient. Consequently, it is obvious that she is designed to be pleasing to men. Further, it is by being pleasing that Rousseau thought a woman avoids subjugation; should she try to become like men, she will fall short and be shown to be inferior.

Thus a female requires a categorically different (i.e., discriminatory) edu-cation. Corresponding to the perceived difference in character, Rousseau proposed a program geared toward producing female dependency such that some means of restraint be established: Up to the age of reason, all little girls need to know is that what they are told to do is good, while what they are for-bidden is bad. "Almost as soon as they can understand what is being said to them, they can be controlled by telling them what people think of them. It would be foolish to speak that way to little boys . . . ."[2] As to the particulars of the education to be given, a female makes the best progress in matters of conduct and taste. So she may be taught needlework, though not in order to give artistic form to spiritual essence. Rousseau specifies lacemaking because it calls for a pleasing pose.[3]

Apparently Rousseau did not think women totally incapable of thought. However, he questioned whether exercising reason is compatible with a woman's "becoming simplicity." Reason, he suggested, is that which brings a person to a knowledge of duties. Thus a woman has occasion to use it and so must be capable of it, though the reasoning required is apparently not com-plex. She need only use it to recognize the natural consequences of her posi-tion: her duty to her husband and her children. From this line of reasoning comes the view that "the ideal woman's mind is pleasing but not brilliant, solid but not deep."[4]

In response to this apparent justification for Rousseau's program, one might be tempted to argue that if there are any causal relationships, it is women's sociological and psychological conditioning that yields perceived character differences, not women's biology. As a result of programs utilizing Rousseau's views, women as girls have been conditioned to respond to the desires and pleasures of men. Consequently, women will not be inclined to compete with men. As Betty Friedan noted, "Two out of three girls who entered college were dropping out before they were finished. In the 1950's, those who stayed, even the most stable, showed no signs of wanting to be anything more than suburban housewives and mothers."[5] Therefore, women need a separate education, but not due to biological differences. A separate educa-tion is needed to overcome the disadvantages of being a female in a culture based on male authority and domination. Only in this way will a woman's intellectual potential develop fully.

ALL-WOMEN'S COLLEGES

Following this line of thought, one might advocate a return to all-women's colleges. Once the wrongs have been offset and there is a generation or two of women who have not been reared in a society with the prevailing values of this one, a mixed classroom will be acceptable. After all, it was only with the establishment of women's colleges that at least half of Rousseau's program for women was challenged. These colleges promoted the intellectual development of women, even if it was primarily to produce better mates for future husbands.

Yet such separation is no longer feasible. Apparently the benefit seen in all-women's colleges today is that a separate environment will enable women to develop academically. Presumably, if men are around, a woman will be encouraged to do no better than average or even mediocre work because women are conditioned against appearing superior. Or perhaps the idea is that if men are around, a woman will likely defer, remaining silent and not asking questions to further her thoughts. Suppose this is true. What is to guarantee that women who have graduated from such colleges will vie with men in their chosen field if they have not had to deal with men before? In fact, one might argue, women need to be in classrooms with men to prepare themselves.

Now there are counters to this argument. For example, in one study it was found that between 1910 and 1960 there was a statistically greater output of achievers among women graduating from all-women's colleges than among women graduating from coeducational institutions.[6] However, it must be noted that the main source of this difference was attributed to the fact that there was a higher percentage of women faculty members and administrators, that is, active role models, in the all-women's colleges. This implies not a need for all-women's colleges, but rather a need for a greater number of career women active in any college woman's life, demonstrating that achievement possibilities are rational alternatives.

In this same study an additional source of the difference in achievement between these groups of women is offered: as the percentage of male students increased, the percentage of women achievers decreased proportionately. This suggests a prima facie advantage to all-women's colleges, since more achievers emerge from a male-free atmosphere than from one shared with men. However it is not clear just what that advantage is. It may be that high achievers coming out of all-women's colleges were seen as "exceptions," by themselves and others, and, as a consequence, their individual capabilities did not change suppositions about women in general. One wonders whether they helped to pave the way for others to follow, or if they even encouraged their daughters to do what they themselves did. Increasing the number of women achievers by a few is not enough, especially if these women do not improve conditions for other women.

Moreover, if all-women's colleges truly were the answer to current problems, one would expect that such colleges would not have witnessed the 1950's decline in achievement documented by Betty Friedan.[7] All-women's colleges may serve to separate women from men, but they are not immune to prevailing societal valuations. For there to be substantive change in the actions of women in general, there must be a change in the attitudes of society. And that requires a change in the attitudes of men. Certainly more effort is involved in confronting and dealing with unaware or unwilling males than is involved in just working with particular women. But to separate women off into all-women's colleges is to leave such things as the Ivy-league tradition, with its power, paternalism, and patriarchalism, untouched. Hence, such a program is not a feasible option for educating women to full potential, productivity, and autonomy.

WOMEN'S STUDIES DEPARTMENTS

Given that there is tentative agreement, one might be tempted to encourage the establishment of departments of Women's Studies at universities as a means of countering the trend in education fostered by Rousseau. This too is unacceptable. Clearly there is a need for Women's Studies; I will not belabor the point. The gross omission of women from history and the other humanities as well as the absurd stereotyping of women by the sciences and the recognized arts is obvious to all who are even the least bit sensitive. (And such stereotyping must be challenged if women are to conceive rational alternatives.) The issue is whether in particular *departments* of women's studies are needed, for there are critical academic considerations involved.

Women's Studies has, of course, resulted in new material. There is growing excitement about what human history will look like once emerging information about white women and Third World people is included in proper perspective. In addition, exciting new techniques are developing such as that of oral history. Prevailing standards of artistic form are being challenged by, for example, the concept of diaries as a public literary medium. Different perspectives are being acknowledged or created regarding the work of recognized scholars. And finally it is becoming clear that objectivity really does amount to a relativity of location and frame of reference of the perceiver such that alternative reference points are being accepted as valuable in and of themselves.

Clearly Women's Studies is substantive, and consequently one might be tempted to argue that a separate department of Women's Studies is needed and that Women's Studies courses are not "parasitic" on traditional disciplines. Just as sociology turned out to be a unique discipline, not covered by history and economics for example, what could come out of a Women's Studies department has yet to be explored. Surely a separate academic discipline will arise from which rational alternatives for women will emerge.

There are defects in this line of thought. In the first place, the information being made available by those doing research in Women's Studies should be regular material important to any department. Creating a special department would channel Women's Studies material away from the curriculum of other departments, making it available to fewer students.

Moreover, specialization has reached absurd extremes, and a separate Women's Studies department would swell rather than stem the tide, perpetuating the helplessness of specialization. Faculty working in Women's Studies and located in the traditional departments are aware of a dependency on each other for material outside their own field. But such information would eventually cease to be readily available if a separate Women's Studies department were established.

Finally, and most important, Women's Studies is not a specialty. It did not evolve as a new topic but arose in response to gross omissions and distortions in the form as well as the content of the traditional disciplines. For example, a course in women's history is designed to fill the gaps and correct the interpretations in male history. Moving such a course off by itself would defeat that purpose. To foster a view that Women's Studies is a new field is to leave the tradition untouched and hence fails to confront the problem.

A second line of reasoning views the overall program of Women's Studies as greater than the sum of its particular parts. Thus many argue that a separate department is needed to foster the larger perspective, not because there is a new topic, but precisely because Women's Studies challenges academia's perspective. However, such work must continue on a small scale within all the departments and should not be determined in advance by a bureaucracy. The large-scale implications will follow of their own accord.

Finally there is a political consideration: it is argued that a department will yield a power base. Power is needed both to initiate change from misogynist material and to ensure the permanence of Women's Studies.

Such considerations, of course, must ultimately be made in terms of particular campuses. However, currently there is some pressure on most departments to reform, for example, by including at least one Women's Studies course, being more selective about materials used, and permitting students to do independent research on Women's Studies topics. This pressure is due in part to affirmative action and in part to a desire to increase enrollment. But if a Women's Studies department were created, such efforts would be perceived as a duplication, and most faculty would regard any possible need as having been provided for, ceasing to feel responsible.

Further, how would such a department be treated? It could hardly have any political clout, especially in matters of budgetary allocations claiming university resources. At best, it would be treated as are departments of home economics — off in a corner where women "do their thing" while men proceed with the "real" work. Should a department of Women's Studies effectively persist at this time, it will be because it is permitted to. Hence, a special department would be no more secure than that of an area studies program; it will not change women's political impotence.

To be effective, Women's Studies must flourish by confronting what exists rather than being put forward as an alternative to what exists. One might think all that is necessary to institute change is to conceive an alternative and show it to be superior. But this, to which history is a frustrated witness, is not the way things work.

MULTIDISCIPLINARY OR AREA STUDIES PROGRAMS

What is needed is a multidisciplinary program, loosely structured and staffed by a coordinator to facilitate exchange of information by faculty teaching and doing research in Women's Studies from within the traditional departments, enabling students to major in Women's Studies. One might wonder at the difference between a Women's Studies department and a multidisciplinary or area studies program, besides the technical matter of the department under which a student is listed. In fact, the difference is considerable.

In the first place, an area studies program will make it possible for material from Women's Studies courses to be integrated into the different disciplines. For example, majors in philosophy will have access to Women's Studies material in the philosophy department and will be able to use it in other courses in that department. And the faculty itself might be exposed to the material. At any rate, ignorance will soon cease to be an excuse.

Secondly, if there is to be a successful turning point in the trend toward specialization, which has reached an absurd extreme — people within one department do not even know or understand what many of their colleagues are doing, much less have a working knowledge of material in other departments — it will be through such area studies programs. Faculty doing research in Women's Studies need each other's information and so will find the time to learn about each other's work. Further, students majoring in Women's Studies will have a good cross-sampling of academic material — something akin to the original conception of the Bachelor of Arts degree.

Thirdly, as members of the traditional departments, Women's Studies faculty would pursue research within these departments. This, if anything, will dispel the illusion that Women's Studies is a specialty. And this is the only way effective critical examination of assumptions held about women will occur. Women's Studies material and faculty must be in a position to challenge the tradition and not be ignored by it.

Finally, if Women's Studies faculty were located in separate departments, all concerned would be encouraged to meet informally outside the academic structure. Students and staff could offer input to faculty and administrators, and an atmosphere of actual exchange and two-way learning might result.

THE WOMEN'S STUDIES STUDENT

However, there is a further, more subtle difference that involves a particularly debilitating attitude toward women. One will recall that in addition to promoting the noneducation of women, Rousseau also promoted female dependency. Rousseau alleged that to avoid subjugation, women must be pleasing to men. One sees now that this is actually a disguised formula for subjugating women. Although women are treated favorably on Rousseau's program — that is, women are not treated with contempt — it is only because in directing effort toward pleasing a man, a woman abdicates autonomy. The most disabling part of Rousseau's program closed to women the development of an independent, autonomous will and the dependency on self as the major source of validation.

Behind the program for all-women's colleges, and to a lesser extent, separate departments of Women's Studies, is often the notion that women need to be reeducated if not reconditioned, so that the best results will obtain if women develop in a protective atmosphere. That is, in order to avoid subjugation, women need special education. Women need to be kept apart from men and to consider themselves different from men. But this is precisely Rousseau's thesis in disguise.

The concept of women as having been conditioned into inferiority and underachievement, and so needing to be reconditioned into equality, is a popular one deriving from the conditioning line in science initiated by Pavlov and developed by Skinnerian behaviorism. It has been used by many concerned to "explain" women's past situations. Roughly, the approach portrays actions of women as caused by antecedent stimuli rather than proceeding from intentional choices. It is important to resist the idea that women have been conditioned to dependency and instead to perceive women as having made rational choices, given available alternatives. If a woman is cunning, it is a quality she developed in compensation not for her lesser strength, but for her lesser power, her lack of autonomy, a lack which calls for manipulation of those who have power in order to obtain her own security.

The difference between accepting the conditioning line and adopting a more rationalistic, intentionalistic analysis is the difference between treating a woman as an object and treating her as a person. Removing a woman's dependency by counter-conditioning, especially when that involves protection, constitutes another doing for a woman what she should do for herself. This does not countermand but rather encourages dependency.[8] Further, any person who is protected will accept subjugation willingly unless he or she is able to see it as problematic by having alternatives available. Otherwise the rational choice is dependency.

Considering the alternatives that have been available, many women not only have not been prepared to think in terms of self-direction, but likely have deep-seated yearnings for someone to come along who will take on that burden and responsibility. To be able to face and deal with this is of utmost importance. But that is not possible so long as there is another well-meaning group acting as a shield. So long as a woman is given protective treatment, treatment of the sort accorded a perceived inferior, she will only seek to please, thus failing to function autonomously. Further, in a protective atmosphere women who challenge the status quo will have a propensity to see themselves as exceptions and so are less likely to encourage others. On the other hand, those challenging in a less protective atmosphere are more likely to regard themselves as fighters and so realize the need to support others.

What is wanted is not protection but respect. Respect is not something given one considered an inferior. One might be pleasantly surprised at a development in a child, but that is not respect. On the other hand, respect is not something given one considered far superior either. In this case, one stands in awe, one does not respect. One who believes in the existence of God, for example, does not respect God. This is not to say that one *dis*respects in either case but rather that the question of respect simply does not arise. Respect is something one must be competent to give as well as competent to receive.

The picture Pousseau portrayed of women might stem from all the love in the world, but it shows no respect; it is not an exchange between equals. And the idea of encouraging all-women's colleges or Women's Studies departments in order to foster a special atmosphere to protect and shield embraces a similar lack of respect. It endorses protection and so encourages dependency.

In sum, Rousseau promoted the noneducation and dependency of women, claiming that character differences between men and women were grounded in biology. One might be tempted today to claim that insofar as they exist, those differences result from conditioning.

Thus the feasibility of looking to all-women's colleges to change the trend in women's education set by Rousseau was considered. It was dismissed because even if more achievers come out of all-women's colleges, it is not clear either that such colleges are immune to prevailing valuations of women or that a few additional "exceptional" achievers will affect those valuations. Similarly, the creation of departments of Women's Studies was dismissed. Women's Studies is not a specialty. It will eventually affect all the academic disciplines. What is acceptable, if Women's Studies is to bring actual change and not perpetuate the academic status quo (either through omission or commission), are multidisciplinary or area studies programs which retain the material in the traditional departments.

Finally, problems with the conditioning line were discussed. If women are to be educated to full potential, women's choices in the past must be perceived as rational, and alternatives must be provided which allow a woman the possibility of seeing herself as part of an ongoing process and not as a freak (albeit an exceptional one). As long as the conditioned view of women persists, dependency will also, perpetuating the status quo. Thus, in working on long-range plans for Women's Studies, not only must one attend to the curriculum and the program as a whole, but there is need also to be mindful of the attitude toward women descending from Rousseau.

NOTES

1. Appreciation is expressed to women attending the Women's Studies session of the 1976 Annual Meeting of the Western Social Science Association and members of the Society for Women in Philosophy, Gwen Dooley and Julia Stanley.

2. William Boyd (trans. and ed.), *The Emile of J. J. Rousseau* (New York: Teachers College Press, 1971), p. 135.

3. *Ibid.*, p. 149.

4. *Ibid.*, pp. 149-50.

5. Betty Friedan, *The Feminine Mystique* (New York: Dell, 1972), p. 142.

6. M. Elizabeth Tidball, "Perspectives on Academic Women and Affirmative Action," *Educational Record*, vol. 54, no. 1 (Spring 1973), pp. 130-36.

7. See Friedan, *op. cit.*

8. For other problems surrounding the conditioned view of women, see Redstockings, "Consequences of the Conditioning Line," *Feminist Revolution* (New Paltz, N. Y.: By the Authors, P.O. Box 413, 1975), pp. 54-59.

ELLEN BONEPARTH
San Jose State University

Evaluating Women's Studies:
Academic Theory and Practice

Evaluation of Women's Studies programs necessarily involves complex and fascinating issues. To what extent do Women's Studies programs meet student needs? Do attitudes, learning, and behavior change through exposure to Women's Studies? If so, can these changes be measured? How do Women's Studies contribute to our general understanding of the human community? Evaluations have tended to focus on the practical accomplishments of Women's Studies programs, such as the appeal of new curricula and attitude changes resulting from involvement with Women's Studies.[1] As a result, insufficient attention has been paid to theoretical issues posed by the development of a new academic discipline.[2] This article begins to remedy this situation by articulating some theoretical concerns and suggesting some approaches to evaluating the academic contributions of Women's Studies programs.

The motivation for analyzing these issues springs from the experience of developing a Women's Studies program at San Jose State University (SJSU), San Jose, California. The program began its fifth year in 1976. Like sister Women's Studies programs throughout the nation, it is still feeling growing pains while nonetheless having become established on the campus. At SJSU, the time has come to step back and consider, in a theoretical sense, where the program is, where it should be heading, and how to get from here to there. It is hoped that an analysis of the SJSU experience, both its successes and its failures, will add insight to some of the dilemmas facing all Women's Studies programs.

WHY WOMEN'S STUDIES?

From a theoretical standpoint, the preliminary question to be asked is "Why establish a women's studies program?" Over time, advocates of Women's Studies have come to answer this question with increasing sophistication. The initial response in the late 1960's was phrased in compensatory terms with the assertion that women, whether as actors or subjects, have been ignored in the evolution of knowledge. It was soon clear that sins of omission are compounded by sins of commission. Scholars have discovered that when the vow of silence is lifted from the topic of women, women are often misunderstood, misrepresented, or mystified. Thus, the case of Women's Studies is phrased in remedial as well as compensatory terms.

Contemporary justifications for Women's Studies go beyond assertions of the need for knowledge about women to assertions of the need for the creation of knowledge by and for women. It is argued that women can bring to scholarship new perspectives and values. While the debate continues as to whether or not these new perspectives and values are unique to females, it is clear that women, as a result of their subordinate place in the academy as well as society, are in a compelling position to ask fundamental questions about "accepted" ideas and thinking. Finally, the justification for Women's Studies is based on the need to provide meaningful educational experiences for female students searching out their own identities. Knowledge for women is as important as knowledge by women. For many students, Women's Studies satisfies the demand for relevance which, when carefully integrated into the curriculum, provides the vitality necessary for an engaging academic career.

The rationale for Women's Studies at SJSU has expanded along with the actual offerings of the program. The invisibility and misrepresentation of women provide ongoing incentives to reexamine the current state of knowledge. The special contributions of women as students, teachers, and scholars provide the impetus for Women's Studies to continue to expand into new areas and concerns.

THE CONTENT OF A WOMEN'S STUDIES PROGRAM

What, then, should be the content of a women's studies program? Ideally, this question should be resolved before instituting a Women's Studies program. Yet the realities of new program development make it virtually impossible to resolve all large theoretical questions in advance. First, the very newness of Women's Studies dictates that programs evolve out of ideas and approaches that must be tried and tested before attaining academic validity. Secondly, the demand for Women's Studies burst forth with great momentum in the context of a burgeoning social movement. The response has necessarily been rapid in order to meet strongly felt needs. Thirdly, Women's Studies programs have typically had to face a relatively hostile environment including some, if not all, of the following elements: administrative resistance to innovation; skepticism and resentment from traditional academic disciplines; scarcity of resources; and the many faces of institutionalized sexism on the campus. Finally, the difficulties of finding consensus on the large, abstract issue of content make it compelling to deal first with smaller, more specific issues of program development.

The question of content in the SJSU Women's Studies Program has not been completely sidestepped, but neither has it been tackled head-on. The question of content surfaces most often in the discussion of course curricula and teaching methods. However, there is a need for a focused discussion of content in order to provide a framework for day-to-day decision-making. An initial evaluation session raised a number of provocative points, elaborated below under four principal questions.

First, Women's Studies programs are generally labeled interdisciplinary. What do we mean by interdisciplinary? In its most elementary sense, interdisciplinary connotes the idea of multidisciplinary, that is, combining courses from a number of different disciplines into one course of study. At SJSU the traditional disciplines have been successfully motivated to offer courses on women to the extent that there are now 44 courses in 19 different departments under the joint sponsorship of Women's Studies and the individual department. The rationale for the multidisciplinary approach is clear: the traditional disciplines have universally ignored women and have failed to integrate the study of women into their course offerings. Therefore, outside efforts to push the disciplines into a concern with women are necessary and well spent.

However, interdisciplinary suggests more than expanding courses in traditional disciplines to include courses on women and combining those courses into one program. Put simply, interdisciplinary suggests that the whole is greater than the sum of its parts. For this reason, four independent Women's Studies courses are offered at SJSU which have no formal link to any department. Clearly, there are informal links as Women's Studies instructors and materials have their origins in traditional academic disciplines. The mere choice of instructors and materials will necessarily emphasize some approaches over others. For example, the choice at SJSU of Women's Studies instructors from history and anthropology has injected a social science emphasis into general Women's Studies courses, while possibly slighting Women's Studies materials from the humanities. Yet, despite such inevitable choices, the principle of creating a new and broader perspective by uniting content from numerous fields holds.

Second, what purposes can be served by creating an interdisciplinary program in which the whole is larger than the sum of its parts? At least three purposes are evident. One can develop an overview of the role of women which merges the limited concerns of specialized fields into a general perspective. Or one can explore the interstices of related fields to draw out the truths that lie between disciplines. Finally, one can develop comprehensive approaches to problem-solving which apply new-found knowledge to old and new problems.

Once Women's Studies programs reach a consensus on these and/or other purposes, they can develop strategies to achieve them. Perhaps, an overview can best be attained by offering students courses combining lectures on a common theme from a variety of traditional academic disciplines. At SJSU, an experimental introductory course on sex roles involving the participation of a number of Women's Studies faculty from the liberal arts, natural sciences, and social sciences is being developed. Perhaps the interstices can best be explored through team-taught courses in related fields. Or, perhaps new methods of problem-solving can best be formulated through courses organized around student or class projects. The point is that program decisions become clearer and easier when they are made with specific interdisciplinary goals in mind.

Another thread running through initial discussions of program content involves the actual rationale for Women's Studies. Clearly, the reasons for involvement in Women's Studies may be as varied and numerous as the people in the program. Participants are united by their common concern with women. The question remains whether that concern with women rests with learning or extends to doing, to changing women's lives. Even the concern with learning about women poses challenges.

A third question to consider is to what extent should a Women's Studies program be oriented toward self-learning or learning about others, toward consciousness-raising or scholarship? The emphasis at SJSU has been placed on scholarship. Given the many opportunities both within and outside the academic community for self-learning through consciousness-raising activities, faculty members tend to see their particular contribution in terms of teaching and research. Moreover, most of our students share an academic orientation to Women's Studies. Clearly, the raising of consciousness takes place in the program, but it occurs as a latent function of the formal educational process, not as an explicit politicizing process.[3] It is important to stress that Women's Studies programs operating in a different type of environment might well view the consciousness-raising process as a necessary element of the academic program. In either case, it is important that Women's Studies programs choose between making consciousness-raising a manifest or latent educational goal.

Finally, in such a setting, what should the role of Women's Studies be? To what extent should Women's Studies programs commit themselves to effect change? Does the study of female oppression demand the effort to eliminate it? Indeed, it seems that a critical difference between Women's Studies and traditional disciplines lies in the commitment of Women's Studies to change and to the idea that learning is only the first step to doing.

The tension between self-learning and learning about others is probably more easily resolved than the tension between pure learning and learning directed to change, between academic activity and political activity, using the word "political" in its broadest sense to mean the use of power to effect change.[4] Traditional disciplines occasionally come under attack for their indifference or insensitivity to political issues. While some actors regularly engage in efforts to bring politics to the university environment, the dictates of professionalism, namely, political neutrality, prevail.

While it is relatively easy to foster learning in the university environment, it is difficult to foster doing. At SJSU, relatively successful learning strategies have been developed, but the search for ways of translating learning into doing is only beginning. While many creative teaching techniques (individual, group, and class projects, guest lectures, field trips, and internships) are used, doing is only sporadically structured into the program. In part, the problem lies in the constraints placed on Women's Studies by the norms of the university. But in part, the problem also lies in liberating the faculty from their own traditionalism in order to devise educational techniques which integrate learning and doing. For example, in a course on women and politics, the present author treats the critical problems of female political socialization and participation, of organizing women, and of influencing public policy affecting women but has yet to evolve teaching techniques that deal with these problems through doing, namely, by providing students with opportunities to organize, elect, lobby, and work for women.

Without opportunities for doing, utilized where they already exist or created where they do not, Women's Studies programs may, despite innovative academic orientations, perpetuate the status quo. While there can be no uniform approach to change-oriented learning, the unique quality of Women's Studies lies in its commitment to change. Essentially, Women's Studies programs must follow both inside and outside strategies that foster learning within the university's walls while continually promoting opportunities to effect change beyond the university environment.

THE CONTENT OF WOMEN'S STUDIES COURSES

In addition to evaluating the content of Women's Studies programs generally, the content of individual Women's Studies courses also needs examination. Here, three sets of questions should be asked.

First, is a course which concerns itself with women by definition a Women's Studies course, or must there be unique features that distinguish Women's Studies courses from traditional course offerings? This question surfaces periodically at SJSU, often as a result of student criticism that some courses fail to address feminist concerns. As a result, a student-faculty committee took on the task of defining criteria for Women's Studies courses.

The committee defined Women's Studies courses as courses "taught from a feminist perspective." Course criteria cover three general areas: research, methodology, and the raising of new questions. The criteria are operationalized as follows:

(1) Looking at new and old research about women;
(2) Raising new questions that are relevant to women;
(3) Raising questions about the silence of traditional disciplines about women;
(4) Raising questions about the male orientation and methodology of traditional fields;
(5) Raising questions about sex role relationships;
(6) Questioning basic assumptions about society;
(7) Encouraging students and faculty to do research on women and to share it with others.

With these criteria in mind, a review of course offerings in individual departments is planned for SJSU. The aim is not to dictate to instructors or to prescribe course content. Clearly, the stereotyping of content would violate the whole thrust of a Women's Studies program. Rather, the hope is that the acceptance of these criteria by instructors will further set off Women's Studies from traditional, male-oriented perspectives on knowledge and will heighten the rigor of course offerings.

Second, in light of the recent outpouring of interest in men's liberation, the question must be asked to what extent should Women's Studies courses concern themselves with men? In discussions at SJSU, there was little agreement on this issue. Some discussants argued that since men were the main subjects of concern in traditional disciplines, it would be totally inappropriate for Women's Studies to devote time to men. Others commented that while men face certain dilemmas in contemporary society, they are not an oppressed group and therefore have no place in the study of oppression. Still others argued that the study of men was necessary in order to liberate both sexes and to provide both men and women with new values for living in relation to each other, whether together or apart.

The place of men as students, instructors, and subjects has not been fully aired in the SJSU Women's Studies program. In practice, male students are generally appreciated and interested male faculty are generally tolerated, while men as subjects are studied only as they are relevant to understanding sex roles. This approach has been viable because few men are knocking down doors to participate in the program. However, some important questions must be raised about this policy of benign neglect. First, is it not a disservice to women to fail to promote their accomplishments, both scholarly and political, before the opposite sex? Secondly, by excluding male concerns from courses, are Women's Studies programs pursuing separatism by default, as well as limiting their possible constituencies? Finally, might the shunting aside of men result in raising up half the world to the incomprehension of the rest?

Lastly, in a similar vein, to what extent should Women's Studies courses concern themselves with sexuality? Certainly, the nature of female sexuality, male-defined sexuality as a form of oppression, and varying forms of sexuality are all questions that lend themselves to academic exploration. In particular, lesbianism has gained recognition in Women's Studies not only as a legitimate individual lifestyle, but also as a viable personal and political alternative to sexism. At the same time, sexual issues continue to provoke controversy on and off the campus and have, in some instances, polarized Women's Studies programs. While a concern with sexuality needs to be integrated into Women's Studies, this concern must be balanced against the right to privacy and, frankly, against the possibilities of political backlash. For Women's Studies programs to pretend that sexuality is noncontroversial is to depart from reality; for Women's Studies programs to evade sexual issues is to continue female repression as well as oppression.

As Women's Studies courses evolve, other questions relating to course content will arise. Continuing evaluation of course content is necessary to stimulate both creativity and continuity. While spontaneity must not be sacrificed to self-consciousness, neither must intellectual rigor be sacrificed to novelty.

THE FUTURE OF WOMEN'S STUDIES

The most compelling issues of all concern the future of Women's Studies. Should the ultimate goal of Women's Studies be integration into the traditional fields, or should it be the development of a unique program to live permanently alongside the traditional disciplines? While this question need not be resolved in the near future, as Women's Studies programs as they now exist have enormous tasks before them, it nevertheless raises some important middle-range strategic considerations. For example, if the ultimate goal of Women's Studies is to self-destruct, then increasing emphasis should be placed on developing materials and courses which integrate Women's Studies into traditional fields. If, on the other hand, the goal is to become established permanently on the campus, Women's Studies programs must move toward undergraduate majors and full-scale graduate programs.

Some will argue that the resolution of this issue lies not in an either/or choice, but rather in a two-pronged approach in which Women's Studies programs seek both to inject their concerns into the traditional disciplines and to maintain their independence. There are at least two difficulties with this approach. First, the situation which most Women's Studies programs face of scarce resources (primarily faculty time and administrative support) raises the strong possibility that in trying to achieve both goals, Women's Studies will fail to achieve either. Secondly, by promoting the uniqueness of Women's Studies to students and then failing to develop full-scale academic programs for them, Women's Studies may be guilty of raising expectations that cannot be met. Again, there is probably no one appropriate solution for all Women's Studies programs. In fact, Women's Studies may have its greatest impact by pursuing integration on some campuses and independence on others. However, the failure of any Women's Studies program to consider its ultimate goals may result in decisions made by default rather than by its own determinations.

At SJSU, problems related to the future of Women's Studies have already surfaced. While the university administration has been supportive of Women's Studies, difficulties have arisen from the fact that the program has not been granted the power to offer tenure-track positions. Recruitment is made much more difficult, and continuity suffers when the program can only offer temporary one-year appointments. Furthermore, an academic program has less security than a full-fledged department and is therefore more vulnerable to mergers with other programs or to even being phased out in the event of a severe decline in student enrollments. Fortunately, growing student enrollments provide a tenable position from which to oppose adverse moves, but it is clear that the program's existence would be more secure with departmental status.

Women's Studies students at SJSU may pursue a minor in Women's Studies at the undergraduate level and a master's degree in social science with an emphasis in Women's Studies at the graduate level. Graduate work in Women's Studies can provide specialized training for careers in many fields in and outside academia. Nonacademic careers would include such things as government work in local, state, national, or international agencies; business consulting; administration of affirmative action programs; publishing, and journalism. Academic careers, of very limited availability at present, include teaching, research, and university administration. Graduate students today are legitimately concerned about the applicability of their studies to future careers. Unless Women's Studies programs become fully institutionalized, there will only be a small number of academic positions available to them.

Thus, there is the temptation to push for a full-scale Women's Studies program which would have the same status as the traditional disciplines. However, it seems likely that once Women's Studies programs become fully institutionalized, vested interests will weaken any commitment to integration into other fields and may make it impossible ultimately to self-destruct if that is the desired goal.

EVALUATION TECHNIQUES

While the discussion of these theoretical issues is in itself an aspect of the evaluation process, explicit ways of evaluating academic practice must be considered. A commitment to innovation in curricula and teaching techniques must be carried over to the evaluation process itself. Surveys of student characteristics and attitudes provide important feedback on many questions, but alternative evaluation techniques are needed to get at the theoretical issues raised here.

In order to assess the value of differing interdisciplinary approaches, an experimental design should be used in which courses oriented toward overview, interrelationships and problem-solving are introduced and compared. Which kinds of courses, such as survey, team-taught, or project-oriented, best succeed in bringing out the interdisciplinary nature of Women's Studies? While student assessments are valuable, it is especially important for instructors to engage in ongoing reviews of the experimental courses they are teaching. Faculty members, as well as students, might keep journals that analyze on a regular basis the value of different course materials, the quality of class discussion, and the substantive areas in which new questions, issues, and solutions are examined. From these journals, a course evaluation can be prepared which would analyze in detail the fruitfulness of different approaches and provide needed guides to future course development.

An experimental approach also seems well suited to an evaluation of the place of men and male concerns in Women's Studies programs. Two similar introductory courses, one focusing exclusively on women and one including male perspectives on sexism, might be offered. Does the inclusion of male concerns enrich or dilute the course, advance or interfere with consciousness-raising, attract or discourage male and female students from enrolling? In such an experiment it would also be worthwhile to examine the extent of attitude change among students as a way of assessing the impact of a female emphasis versus a female-and-male emphasis.

Traditional student evaluations are probably the best technique for judging the extent to which courses are taught from a feminist perspective. Because beginning students may not be fully prepared to make such judgments, advanced or graduate students should also participate in this process, as they have a greater familiarity with the content of Women's Studies and can therefore provide more meaningful inputs. These inputs might be discussed in faculty-student symposia in order that instructors might benefit from exposure to new ideas, and students might benefit from exposure to teaching methods that they themselves might use in their own teaching efforts.

Lastly, follow-up interviews with students may be the best way to analyze the value of learning through doing. What changes occur in students' personal lives, activities, and politics (again, in the largest sense of the word) as a result of exposure to Women's Studies? Has the Women's Studies program been successful in opening up vistas and preparing students to challenge the traditional patterns of the "real world"? Or has the program raised their expectations to the point that they only meet frustration in efforts to change their lives? Or, worse yet, do they end up concluding that what they have learned in Women's Studies has no significance for the "real world"? Such questions cannot be fully explored in mail questionnaires or surveys. While students cannot be compelled to share their experiences, many would respond positively to meeting with faculty individually or in groups in order to help further the goals of Women's Studies programs.

Poet Adrienne Rich has described Women's Studies as "an alternate mode of thinking . . . not an appendage to the real curriculum but a questioning of the nature of knowledge itself."[5] In undertaking such a large endeavor, it is crucial not only to stop periodically to ask hard theoretical questions and to answer them with the greatest candor, but also to appreciate that evaluation is an ongoing process with changing questions and answers. Creative evaluation techniques are an effective way of bringing academic theory and practice together.

NOTES

1. Two conferences held at Wesleyan University in 1973 and 1974 were devoted to the problem of evaluating Women's Studies programs. Dr. Marcia Guttentag's "Multi-attribute-utility Decision Theoretical Model of Evaluation," presented at those conferences, has been adapted by a number of universities for evaluation of content, teaching methods, reasons, and results of taking Women's Studies courses.

2. Theoretical issues are raised periodically in the *Women's Studies Newsletter*, vols. I-IV (Old Westbury, N. Y.: The Feminist Press, 1972-76).

3. For an explanation of consciousness-raising as a process, see Anne Koedt *et al., Radical Feminism* (New York: Quadrangle, 1973), pp. 280-89.

4. A somewhat differing conception of the political nature of Women's Studies may be found in Linda Gordon, "A Socialist View of Women's Studies: A Reply to the Editorial, Volume I, Number 1," *Signs*, vol. 1, no. 2 (Winter 1975), p. 565.

5. *California Women in Higher Education Newsletter*, vol. 2, no. 1 (Mar. 1976), p. 4.

MARY STEWART
PAT ERICKSON
University of Missouri–Kansas City

The Sociology of Birth: A Critical Assessment of Theory and Research

Although sociologists have applied their theoretical and analytical abilities to many stages of the life process—childhood, adolescence, transition to marriage and family, widowhood, aging, and death—the life entry stage has been virtually ignored by sociologists. Demographers have traced rates of fertility and fecundity, and anthropologists have given fairly extensive attention to the process of pregnancy and birth in different cultures.[1] The greatest interest in pregnancy and birth has been evidenced by physiologists, embryologists, and pharmacologists, and the bulk of the research appears in such journals as the *American Journal of Nursing, Journal of Psychosomatic Research,* and *Journal of Obstetrics and Gynecology*. Psychologists have not altogether neglected the area of birth, although their concentration on the individual and internal states may be somewhat limited.[2] Even the popular press has been more attentive to pregnancy, labor, and birth than has sociology.[3] A review of the literature, however, indicates that within sociology the attention which has been given this area comes from the deviance theorists' research on illegitimacy or abortion and from the superficial coverage offered by marriage and family literature, which is more likely to discuss the impact of the infant on the extant family. The inevitable conclusion is that there remains a curious lack of interest in birth within the discipline of sociology.

There are various reasons why such an obvious and important area has been neglected within sociology long after the acceptance of a sociological analysis of death, an equally natural and ordinary, albeit more inevitable, process.[4] Perhaps because these events and processes have been taken for granted and have been so intricately woven into the social fabric, they have not been sifted out as something which merits our attention and have thus evaded analysis by researchers. Yet their very pervasiveness, their unquestioned existence, indicates their imposing weight, their importance in the formation of the infrastructure of the social system. Yet why has a phenomenon that is so pervasive become a taken-for-granted reality?

One of the most obvious reasons for the neglect is that pregnancy and birth are experiences specific to women. Furthermore, they are viewed as the natural expression of and integral to being a woman in our society. Those women who do not have these experiences are met with either suspicion or sympathy.

Just as with other experiences or exigencies that are specific to women, pregnancy and birth have not been viewed as significant topics of investigation, relegating them to the role of "women's issues," women's problems, occupying much the same interest as "women's stories" in literature.[5] Feminists have decried the treatment of women by health care experts. Authors such as Seaman[6] and Frankfort[7] not only point out the neglect of women's health issues, but also illustrate the misconceptions about women and their bodies perpetuated by training programs for physicians, especially obstetrics-gynecology practitioners. The neglect of women's health issues has led some feminists to demand that males be denied further entrance to obstetrics-gynecology residencies.[8]

The evidence that suggests that women's health was not a significant factor in the production and proliferation of potentially death-dealing and crippling birth control devices, or that treatment of breast cancer has not been more adapted to women's needs than to the surgeon's skill, or that such female-specific diseases such as endrometriosis have not been investigated for either cause or successful treatment all merely illustrate the politically disenfranchised position of women. The neglect of issues within the sociology of birth provides further evidence of the powerlessness and social insignificance of women.

If we define pregnancy and birth as processes which are inseparable from being a woman, as an extension of the female role, and if these processes are so much a part of the definition of woman as to be her presumed nature, then we cannot even perceptually differentiate them as processes significant for study. The mere fact that pregnancy and birth are processes experienced (at least most intimately and, until recently, almost inevitably) by women has been partially responsible for the neglect of these areas by social scientists. An indication of this is the realization that male-specific or male-related diseases or risks, from prostate problems to impotency and heart failure, have been far more likely to attract the attention and interest of researchers and policymakers. One simply does not gain status by working with processes or problems related to low-status people.

Sociologists, along with economists, historians and psychologists, have paid scant attention to women. There are several reasons for this in addition to the general devaluation of and disinterest in women. First, most sociologists are male and most theorists and methodologists within sociology are male. Consequently, their work, the areas they choose to investigate or analyze, have reflected male interests. In addition, as sociology has become a more specialized field, the areas of specialty not only reflect the selection by male sociologists of what is a significant area of study, but as a consequence provide interest and research in areas in which males have been the primary and most powerful participants.

A glance at the many areas of specialization illustrate this point: Complex Organizations, Occupations and Professions, Industrial Sociology, Sociology of Sports, Criminology, Sociology of Work and Stratification. Women seem to have interested them only if they are deviant in some fashion (lesbian or prostitute) or as they fill their role or prepare for their potential role of a man's wife or someone's mother. Women's lives have not been seen as significant enough to warrant study, with some important exceptions.[9]

Another related consideration within sociology is that on the prestige scale, study of women ranks fairly low. Such areas as marriage and family are most likely to deal with the lives and experiences of women. Yet even in this relatively low status sub-field, males dominate in both research and authorship, while women may be asked to teach the courses because it is consistent with their "nature," interests, or "natural abilities," much as women have been encouraged to enter the compatible professions of nursing, teaching, and, within medicine, pediatrics. Only recently have women abandoned the notion that marriage and family courses must be avoided if one is to be a serious sociologist and have come full circle to the understanding that this area and the topics included therein require the elucidation which can be provided by conscientious women sociologists. Thus, the attempt by sociology to gain acceptance as a significant science and the attempt by sociologists to gain prestige and status within their field contributed to the neglect of issues of pregnancy and birth (women's issues) within the field.

During the past several years, however, significant social changes have provided an atmosphere in which the emergence of a sociology of birth seems more possible. Certainly the Women's Movement has generated an enormous amount of research on women, sex roles, etc., and the specific issues raised by the Women's Movement, such as inadequate health care, oppression by institutions in which women operate, and denial of rights over self, body, and life, have provided a wealth of research topics and have led to the allocation of monies to fund studies. A related movement, which could be termed "back to the earth," ritualistic, reactionary, and mostly antithetical to the Women's Movement, has also focused upon the damage perpetrated upon women by hospitals and their personnel. The interests of the very traditional earth-mother women in this movement, the work of professionals and others in the development of prepared childbirth and encouragement of home births, the inclusion of the father in the pregnancy and the birth process, and the legalization of nurse-midwifery have dovetailed with the criticism being voiced by various segments of the Women's Movement that the medical establishment consistently oppresses, degrades, and damages them through its organizational structure and emergent definitions.

These broad social factors have, it seems, provided a climate in which the sociology of birth can emerge as a legitimate area of study, and indeed a growing number of sociologists in this and other countries are doing research on the life entry process. The sociology of birth can be broadly defined as the application of sociological theory and methodology to that significant life process which chronologically incorporates the period from decision-making through the first year of an infant's life. The possible topics for investigation are numerous, as the field is largely untrammeled and is one which can incorporate such diverse research as the study of "products of the womb" to the changing self-image of the woman throughout the pregnancy stage.[10] The area can be delineated into six stages or phases: (1) the decision to or not to become pregnant, (2) the pregnancy phase, (3) labor and delivery, (4) the post-delivery stage, (5) the first six weeks, and (6) the first year.

The task now is to more clearly delineate this field of study and to provide analysis and areas for analysis. This process may be enhanced by outlining at least one possible form that the sociology of birth might take. In the following discussion, attention will be focused on two of these phases: (1) pregnancy and (2) labor and delivery.

PREGNANCY

In light of the prevalence of the phenomenon of pregnancy, it is surprising to note the paucity of attention and information on the subject within the discipline of sociology. This neglect of the topic of pregnancy is evidenced by the minimal attention given to this phase in marriage and family textbooks as well as by the lack of attention devoted to pregnancy in related journals.

A survey of some of the most widely used texts in the area of marriage and the family discloses either no discussion of the phenomenon of pregnancy[11] or a cursory examination of the subject.[12] Though the subject of children is usually given extensive coverage in such texts, it is often assumed that the transition from pre- to post-parenthood is a relatively smooth one, although there is some recognition of the temporary disruptiveness caused by the infant. Some attention may be given to difficulties or changes experienced during the pregnancy period, such as anxiety about the prospective parent role, but no systematic treatment is offered whereby the social reality of pregnancy is understood.[13]

The sociological research that has been done in the area of pregnancy reveals a narrowness of scope in the analysis of this phenomenon. Miller has classified research in the area of pregnancy as centering about five major themes.[14] First, a social problems orientation exists, where the major focus has been the analysis of deviant pregnancies (e.g., the unwed pregnant teenager). Second, there is a socio-medical orientation, where the major focus is on the "health issues" of pregnancy (e.g., prenatal care, diet, poverty). Third, a personal adjustment theme is stated, where psychoanalytic concepts are applied to pregnancy. Fourth, a social planning focus is defined, which emphasizes a demographic analysis of fecundity and fertility rates and is often concerned with the consequences of "excessive" numbers of births. Fifth, there is an ethnographic approach, which describes pregnancy in various cultures. Miller's bibliography on pregnancy substantiates the classifications presented above.[15]

From these classifications, it is apparent that *sociological* research in the area has been extremely limited in terms of the types of pregnancy "issues" that have been analyzed. For the most part, sociological analysis of pregnancy stems from a deviance or demographic orientation. Outside the discipline of sociology, medical, psychoanalytic, and anthropological orientations predominate. The reasons for this "narrow" treatment of pregnancy within the discipline of sociology have already been discussed. It is the intent in this section to demonstrate the potential benefits of a broader sociological approach through a description of the applicability of role theory to pregnancy. This analysis will primarily focus on some of the "unique" features of the pregnant role and examples of sociological research in the area of pregnancy.

Role Entrance

Traditionally, there have been tremendous cultural pressures for married women to enter the pregnant role. There has also been little that women could do to prevent the physiological reality of pregnancy. With the availability of contraception and the emergence of the Women's Movement, the inevitability and desirability of entrance into the pregnancy role is being seriously questioned by many women. For women who do enter the pregnant role, the mechanisms for entry can vary in terms of whether entrance into the role was planned, accidental, or coerced (e.g., rape). The reactions to and interpretations of the pregnant role may therefore be expected to vary, depending on the mode of entry.

The conditions under which women enter this role can also vary in terms of the legitimacy of role entrance. Normatively, pregnancy has been "reserved" for married women, and there have also been implicit age prescriptions in terms of the appropriate time for the assumption of this role. In contemporary American society, the pregnant teenager or the pregnant woman over forty may be viewed as occupying a deviant role for her age. These traditional definitions of deviant pregnancies are being questioned by an increasing number of women who opt for the adoption of the pregnant role outside the traditional marital structure. The reasons for and consequences of their choice of a deviant role would be an interesting subject for sociological research.

Entrance into the pregnancy role may also be expected to vary by socioeconomic position, race/ethnicity, and religious affiliation. For example, the number of times entrance into this role is considered appropriate and the type of decision-making involved in role entrance may be predicted to vary with each of these three variables.

These considerations indicate that entrance into the pregnant role is an extremely complex process. The analysis of the process is further complicated by the interplay between a physiological reality and a social reality. Entrance into the pregnant role is preceded by a physiological diagnosis of pregnancy, either by self or by an expert. This physiological condition must then be interpreted and translated into a social reality.

Miller questions the assumption of an equivalence between the physiological reality and social reality of pregnancy.[16] She treats the issue of acquiring a pregnancy identity as problematic and focuses on the process through which pregnant women acquire the pregnancy identity and become socially defined as pregnant. Utilizing panel interviews as a basis for analysis, Miller makes a distinction between "true-planners," "sort-of-planners," and "non-planners" in terms of the extent to which their pregnancy was a planned event. The conclusion is that these groups differed in important ways in terms of their acquisition of a pregnancy identity. For example, the non-planners saw physical signs of pregnancy cues only retrospectively — after they had been medically diagnosed as pregnant, while the true and sort-of-planners made their own initial diagnoses. The non-planners entered into use of medical facilities for sickness, not for pregnancy, while the sort-of/true-planners sought obstetrical care. The non-planners had no new identity to reveal to friends, relatives, husbands before diagnoses, while the true and sort-of-planners discussed their probable new identity with others. Finally, the non-planners had a much weaker attachment to their new pregnant status.

In sum, the process of entrance into the pregnant role is one which could benefit from many kinds of sociological analyses, ranging from an examination of the decision-making process and of the structural conditions surrounding entrance into the pregnant role to the acquisition of a pregnancy identity.

Role Expectations

The pregnant role has some unique features associated with it in comparison with other types of roles (e.g., marital, occupational). The pregnant role is one which lasts for a relatively short period of time. Progression in the role is accompanied by a tremendous number of physiological changes, and the most visible of these changes end when the role is terminated. The "successful" completion of the pregnant role results in the immediate acquisition of another role — motherhood. These features of the pregnant role lead one to ask about the set of expectations of that role. How do the temporariness, the physiological manifestations, and the acquisition of a new role when the pregnant role is "successfully" completed affect the set of expectations of the pregnant role?

Rather than assuming that the pregnant role is characterized by role clarity and harmony, the features of the pregnant role described above would lead one to argue that the role is characterized by role ambiguity and inconsistency. The temporariness of the role may mean that there is not sufficient time to feel comfortable in the role. Indeed the temporariness and the knowledge of when the role will terminate may mean that a clear set of expectations for the role have not been completely developed, i.e., it is characterized by role ambiguity.

The physiological changes occurring may be interpreted in a variety of ways. On the one hand, pregnancy may be defined as an illness. Since, in contemporary American society, the appropriate "handling" of a pregnant role requires regular visits to a physician and the termination of the role occurs within a hospital setting, there does exist an "illness" expectation attached to that role. This expectation is intensified by physiological changes which may result in morning sickness, toxemia, etc. The interpretation of this "illness" definition may result in the expectation that other roles of the pregnant woman (e.g., sexual, occupational) should be curtailed or terminated.

On the other hand, pregnancy has been conceptualized as a time during which women reach the "peak" of their femaleness. Such an inconsistent set of expectations not only implies difficulty for the pregnant woman in assessing what behavior is appropriate for the role (sickness or radiant health) but also implies that physiological changes occurring will have consequences for the pregnant woman's self-image.

Finally, Alice Rossi has suggested that although pregnancy is viewed as a time of anticipatory socialization for the role of mother, in comparison with occupational and marital roles, there is a lack of any realistic training for the role of mother. Rossi argues that the preparation time that exists is "confined to reading, consultation with friends and parents, discussions between husband and wife and a minor nesting phase in which a place and the equipment for a baby are prepared in the household."[17]

It is not suggested that all pregnant women will experience role inconsistency and role ambiguity. But rather the degree of role ambiguity and inconsistency will vary in terms of the interpretations that the pregnant women attach to their experience. For example, women who have "successfully" completed several pregnancies may experience less role ambiguity. Women with "problem" pregnancies may accept the illness conceptualization of the role more readily. In addition, the expectations attached to the pregnant role may vary by marital status, socioeconomic position, and race/ethnicity.

For example, women engaged in deviant pregnancies whose financial resources are limited may view the anticipatory socialization expectation of the pregnant role as a source of anxiety. Likewise women who are employed full-time in a career may also view the pregnant role as a cause of anxiety. Therefore, the expectations of the pregnant woman cannot be assumed to be well-defined. Rather the characteristics of the pregnant role outlined above suggest that the pregnant role is characterized by ambiguity and inconsistency and further variations may be anticipated due to differences in marital status, socioeconomic position, and race/ethnicity.

Role Relationships

One of the interesting features of the pregnant role is the degree of isolation the pregnant woman experiences from others who are experiencing the same process. Even if friends happen to be or have been pregnant, it is not likely that these friends will be at the same stage of the pregnancy process. Unlike other preparatory roles (e.g., graduate school), where there emerges a "fellowship of suffering" among those experiencing or enduring the same process, the pregnant woman can share little of her concerns, anxieties, etc., with others who are also in the pregnant role.[18] There is no pregnancy subculture for most women.

Most role relationships of the pregnant woman are therefore with others who are not in the role. These others are likely to be her spouse, friends, relatives, employer, and physician, all of whom have a set of expectations about the pregnant role. Since, as indicated in the last section, the expectations for the pregnant role are ambiguous and inconsistent, it is likely that others' expectations conflict with one another and with the pregnant woman's own set of expectations. Even more significantly, because of the physiological manifestations of pregnancy, the major status variable that others are likely to be typically reacting to is the pregnant one. Hence, the focal identity for others is likely to be the pregnant identity, and other identities of the pregnant woman may not be viewed as relevant and important.

Furthermore, interpretation of her behavior may be linked to her pregnant role. Her emotions may be taken "lightly" by others because they are seen as stemming from her pregnant status.[19] If a woman defines the pregnant role as her most salient role, then no difficulty may arise. However, if other identities are equally or more salient, then the pregnant woman may encounter role strain. For example, La Rossa examined the relationship between first pregnancy, role salience, and marital strain.[20] Using a systems approach, he argued that the degree to which marital partners have occupational versus familial orientations is of critical import in assessing the impact of the first pregnancy on the marital relationship. Where the occupational identity is primary for one or both partners, it is highly likely that the first pregnancy will create a great deal of marital strain, while a familial orientation of both partners lessens the strain of the first pregnancy.

Obviously, the role relationships of the pregnant woman are in need of further analysis and elaboration. For example, how does the socioeconomic position of the pregnant woman affect the relationship she has with her physician? What are the role relationships of women engaged in "deviant" pregnancies? The preceding discussion has illustrated some of the major issues that are open for investigation.

Role Exit

The typical mechanism for exit from the pregnancy role is through the "successful" completion of that role and entry into the role of motherhood. The pregnant woman, however, has little control over the timing for exit from this role, outside of knowing that it will usually end in nine months. Exit from the role in this manner therefore means little control over the termination of one role and entrance into another role.

Exit from the role may also occur before the "successful" completion of the role where the exit is involuntary—miscarriage. Exit in this manner not only means that the pregnant role has been terminated early, but entry into the mother role is no longer a possibility at that time. This "unsuccessful" completion of the role and the lack of control over its termination would be expected to have important implications for definition of self.

Finally, exit from the role may be accomplished through voluntary termination before the "successful" completion of the role through abortion. Abortion as a mode of exit indicates a rejection of the pregnancy and/or motherhood identity. An important question for research is ascertaining under what conditions is abortion as a mode of exit chosen by the pregnant woman. For example, Rosen and Martindale analyzed the relationship between contraception, abortion, and self concept, using data collected on 1,746 women with "problem pregnancies."[21] They concluded that significantly more aborters reported the use of contraception than was true of the group who have the child, and women who had contracepted and/or who had chosen abortion were significantly higher in perceived competence and lower in traditional female role orientations than those who had not contracepted or had not chosen abortion. They interpret these findings as indicating that both a decision to contracept and a decision to abort indicate activism rather than passivity and that among the forces resulting in activism are a sense of competence and a manifest concern for one's own rights.

Rosen and Martindale's analysis provides an assessment of the interplay between mode of entrance, role expectations, and mode of exit. That is, the use of contraception and the rejection of traditional female role is associated with abortion as a mode of exit. Several other research questions concerning the interplay among the various aspects of the pregnant role emerge. For example, if the mode of entrance is coercive, as in rape, what is the probability that the mode of exit will be abortion? Even more significant, what is the socially constructed reality which intervenes between this mode of entry and exit? Or if the mode of entry is planned and the exit is miscarriage, what are the implications for the woman's self-image? These questions suggest that not only is each aspect of the pregnant role, the entrance, expectations, relationships and exit, filled with research possibilities, but also that the relationships among them is an exciting area for inquiry.

LABOR AND DELIVERY

Descriptions of birth experiences vary enormously. Some women recall it as the most gruesome, bloody, and horrible experience of their lives. Others indicate that they had the most satisfying, deepest orgasm during delivery. Surely the manner in which women describe their labor and delivery varies by many factors, including such things as the setting, the difficulty of the labor, their definition of themselves as sick or healthy, their expectations, and how well these were met.

A complete sociological analysis of labor and delivery would take into account such factors as the impact of different organizational settings, role relationships within those settings, support structures, and the impact of such characteristics as socioeconomic status, marital status, definition of the pregnancy as problematic or not, race, and age. All of these would affect both the experience and the interpretation of that experience by self and others. Although there are many research questions to be posed about labor and delivery, one way of delineating the area for investigation is to look at the process of entering the birth setting and then at labor and delivery, recognizing that these would vary by institutional requirements as well as by many other characteristics of self, relationships, and social structure.

Entry

Whether the mother chooses home or hospital birth, she is very likely ill-prepared for the role of mother. Regardless of the number of previous children, there is almost a total lack of knowledge and control over the process of "giving birth," which is one of the most powerful processes many women will ever experience. This failure leaves a woman unprepared for the reality into which she is so quickly and irreversibly thrust, especially if she, like the vast majority of women, enters an institutional setting for labor and delivery.

Beginning with their redefinition in terms of social and biological history upon admission, through the increasing loss of control which they experience as labor becomes heavier, women are transformed from adults with identities to faceless children. The transformation can be rapid because the woman is encouraged to perceive the situation as one of crisis which demands her co-operation. Family members, from whom she will soon be almost entirely isolated, encourage her to submit and cooperate. High status persons on whom she is dependent for information and help also encourage cooperation. This process is similar to the process of becoming a mental patient described so well by Goffman as a process in which the pre-patient cooperates in his/her own capture and is then angry and humiliated for having done so.[22] During this entry phase, the woman is often unaware of procedure, and her lack of knowledge makes her more vulnerable and more dependent on the very people who will prep and drug and otherwise manipulate her for their convenience and for the smooth operation of the institution. It is interesting to note the patient's lack of information, considering that she may have had nine months of contact with an obstetrician, a person quite familiar with hospital procedure. It is plausible that the obstetrician had nothing to gain by informing the patient, since he maintains a separation between the other activities that take place in the labor setting and his more important work of delivering.

Scully and Bart report that our official experts on women, gynecologists, are unbelievably condescending to women, often casting them in roles of frigidity and usually seeing them as narcissistic, masochistic, and passive.[23] These characteristics do not enhance communication with women on an adult level and make meaningful communication with women, who are viewed as driven by their hormones and likely to be emotionally unstable, even less likely.

During contact with the obstetrician and the transition from woman to child, when the change from autonomous decision-maker to dependent begins, role relationships of differential power, authority and knowledge are clearly established, and these ease the transition which is expected in the hospital. Women who walk into hospitals are soon wheeled through the halls in wheelchairs and are assigned a bed in a labor room which may be occupied by several women in various stages of labor and responding quite differently. Whether they are prepped or not, what sort of prep they receive is controlled by the staff according to such factors as hospital policy or financial status. The decision to have drugs, either pain killers or drugs that affect labor, is a decision in which women have only minimal, if any, say. The staff may encourage submission to drugs during their most vulnerable labor times and may cajole and convince when the woman is least resistant and most reliant upon the judgment of others. These others are likely to make decisions based upon organizational requirements, routine practices, or preference rather than the desires or plans of the woman.

A growing awareness of this has led to the questioning of the hospital as an appropriate place for giving birth. In tracing the development of the dependence upon hospitals, researchers have indicated that the process was heavily influenced by political power struggles rather than by concern with improving health care for women during labor and delivery.[24] Women, such as those interviewed by Caterine Milinaire, are rejecting the notion that birth is unnatural and a form of sickness, and they are questioning the institutional treatment of this process as a sickness.[25] Because women in our culture receive extensive obedience training and because their socialization leads to dependence, easy acceptance of guilt, and feelings of inadequacy or incompetence, they are especially vulnerable to degradation by the labor and delivery situation. During a period of pain and powerlessness, they are more susceptible to institutional intervention than they might otherwise be.

Labor and Delivery

It is difficult to separate labor from entry since most women do not enter the hospital until they are well into labor. This is why women who enter hospitals are so vulnerable to institutional requirements. They are involved in a process over which they have less control than they usually have. They anticipate some pain, but they cannot form any clear picture of what lies ahead or how long, or how hard the labor and delivery might be and what the outcome will be. It is reasonable to assume, as did Bernstein, Kinch, and Stern in a study of anxiety and length of labor,[26] and Fox in his study of the relationship between degrees of neuroticism and length of labor, that the length and difficulty of labor may be associated with individual characteristics such as desire to have a child, general tolerance of pain, fear, and definition of pregnancy as a sickness or a healthy state.[27] However, it is more important to look at the interactional and structural factors which may effect both labor and delivery.

The work of such authors as Kovit,[28] Rosengren and Devault[29] and Paige and Paige[30] encourages further analysis of the organizational characteristics and definitions that affect labor and delivery. Just as importantly, the disappointments and experiences of women who have labored and given birth in these institutions encourages further careful research. The description of the almost total objectification of the woman during labor and delivery as "primips," "multips," or as patients who will "precip," "dump" or provide an "interesting or routine or textbook" case, and the determination of such things as length of labor, type of prep, or whether or not to perform Caesarean section by the availability of personnel, changing shifts, work load, need for training, and other obligations is one of the major contributions of Kovit's work.

This coincides directly with women's damning evaluation of their treatment by doctors and nurses, their lack of decision-making ability, and their feelings of powerlessness. Because the woman is experiencing a total institution with all of its control and coercion mechanisms during a period of pain and transition, she is especially susceptible to organizational demands. Furthermore, the very techniques that are viewed as necessary, such as the administration of drugs or strapping down, increase her powerlessness and impair her abilities to control her situation. This process of systematic degradation, the transition from responsible adult to incompetent child, and the ever greater imposition of institutional demands resulting in her increasing powerlessness is worthy of study, both in terms of status degradation and radical resocialization. The oppressive treatment of women in hospitals needs to be examined not only in organizational terms, but also with emphasis on the relationship between the woman's sex-role socialization and the demands placed on her during labor and delivery. The impact of this process; how it relates to her definition of self as capable and competent; and how it affects subsequent feelings about self, the child's father, and the child all need investigation. What is the long-term impact of the experience, whether severe humiliation or exhilaration, on her relationship with others and subsequent treatment of the child or other children?

Despite the fact that most labors and deliveries are not problematic, the establishment of a crisis orientation in hospitals simultaneously leads to and serves as justification for the dehumanization of the patient. The responses to an actual crisis or complication and the factors which effect that response would be an interesting research area. Characteristics of the woman, such as marital status, response to pain, and social status, may be expected to influence the responses to her. In addition, how interesting or informative the case is, how instructive it might be, and other such considerations apparently influence behavior of others toward the woman and thereby interact with the problem.

It would be of some interest to study the degree of pain experienced by women in labor and delivery and their response to it, as these are related to various characteristics of the physical/social setting. The situation, whether it be private and comfortable or crowded and unpleasant, can be expected to affect not only the amount of pain, but also the expression of pain and the woman's feeling about herself because of her response (i.e., shame, guilt, relief, or gratification). Social characteristics of the woman will also affect the situation she is placed in and thereby the other variables and will influence others' responses to her expression of pain. Exploratory interviews suggest that black women, especially young, unmarried black women, may be seen as "deserving" their pain by paying for their sexual misconduct. An interpretation may apply on a more subtle plane to all women: "Women shall give birth in sadness" in payment for original transgression.

The isolation experienced by the woman throughout these processes must be especially severe during delivery. Separation from significant and familiar others during a period of such social consequence is unique to the birth experience. During grave illness, even during death, others are allowed to participate, to oversee, or to merely be present. This physical and social isolation must have significant consequences on the mother's response. The subsequent separation of her from her baby probably increases her feeling of being in a transitional status of having given birth but not yet being a mother socially. A question presents itself: When does a woman define herself as a mother, and what are the structural and interactional factors that affect that definition? This also calls for extensive research, for the questions to be explored are numerous.

IMPLICATIONS FOR FUTURE RESEARCH

In the foregoing sections, discussion has centered on the neglect of the sociology of birth within the discipline of sociology and the reasons why it is an important area for sociological research. Focusing on the areas of pregnancy and labor and delivery, it has been demonstrated that the utilization of sociological perspectives can enhance understanding of each of these areas and point to numerous research possibilities.

It has also been argued that the sociology of birth is not an area limited to pregnancy and the labor and delivery process. The decision to or not to become pregnant, the immediate post-delivery phase, the first six weeks after birth, and the first year are also areas that should be included. Numerous sociological research questions can be asked about these latter four areas. For example, in the area of decision-making, little is known about the pressures to become parents. Pressures are both explicit and implicit from parents, peers, or the media, and these pressures may vary by class, age, sex, religion, and career pattern. In terms of the post-delivery stage, it is important to investigate the factors that affect the parents' initial reaction to the child (e.g., sex of child, immediate contact, behavior of hospital staff, difficulty of labor, or multiple births). For the first six weeks, the focus of investigation could be on the changes in interaction, attitudes which may be the result of the infant's behavior or characteristics (e.g., colicky or irritable) and/or the mother's health (soreness, fatigue) and social situation (physical and social isolation). Finally, the areas to investigate during the first year would include an examination of the parent role in terms of parents' expectations and evaluations of the child, strains caused by the presence of the child, and coping behavior.

In short, it is argued here that the neglect of sociological research in the area of sociology of birth is due not to an absence of research potential, but rather to an explicit and/or subtle unconcern with women's issues. It is hoped that with an awareness of the importance and potential of research in this area, sociologists will begin to apply theoretical perspectives and methodologies to it.

NOTES

1. See Lucille F. Newman, "The Anthropology of Birth," *Sociological Symposium*, vol. 8 (Spring 1972), pp. 51-63, for an elaboration of anthropological contributions.

2. See, for example, Fox's study of the relationship between degree of neuroticism and

length of labor, Warren Fox, "Psychological Factors in Childbirth" (Ph.D. dissertation, New York University, 1964).

3. Niles Newton, "Childbirth and Culture," *Psychology Today*, vol. 4 (Nov. 1970); Richard L. Krebs, "Mother and Child: Interrupters," *Psychology Today*, vol. 3 (Jan. 1970); Melissa Stones, "Giving Birth," *Ramparts*, vol. 13 (Sept. 1974); Boston Women's Health Book Collective, "Woman's Body/Woman's Mind; Post Partum Blue—As Natural As Natural Childbirth," *Ms.*, vol. 4 (Mar. 1976).

4. The earliest and best known study is David Sudnow's *Passing On; The Social Organization of Dying* (Englewood Cliffs, N. J.: Prentice-Hall, 1967).

5. See Elizabeth Hardwick, *Seduction and Betrayal; Women in Literature* (New York: Vintage Books, 1975).

6. Barbara Seaman, "Pelvic Autonomy: Four Proposals," *Social Policy*, vol. 5 (Sept./Oct. 1975), pp. 43-47.

7. Ellen Frankfort, *Vaginal Politics* (New York: Quadrangle, 1972).

8. Seaman, pp. 43-47.

9. For these exceptions, see Jessie Bernard, *Academic Women* (New York: Meridian, New American Library, 1964); Helena Lopata, *Occupation: Housewife* (New York: Oxford University Press, 1971); and Anne Oakley, *Women's Work: The Housewife Past and Present* (New York: Pantheon, 1974).

10. Leonard Kovit, "Babies As Social Products" (paper delivered to the Seventy-first Annual Meeting of the American Sociological Association, New York, Aug. 1976).

11. Rose L. Coser, *The Family; Its Structure and Functions* (New York: St. Martin's Press, 1964); Robert F. Winch, *The Modern Family* (New York: Holt, Rinehart and Winston, 1963).

12. Bert N. Adams, *The American Family* (Chicago: Markham Publishing Co., 1971); Robert R. Bell, *Marriage and Family Interaction* (Homewood, Ill.: Dorsey Press, 1971); Carolyn C. Perrucci and Dena B. Targ, *Marriage and the Family; A Critical Analysis and Proposals for Change* (New York: David McKay, 1974); Ira L. Reis, *The Family System in America* (New York: Holt, Rinehart and Winston, 1971); Arlene S. Skolnick and Jerome H. Skolnick, *Family in Transition* (Boston: Little, Brown, 1971).

13. Bell, pp. 423-26.

14. Rita Seiden Miller, "The Social Construction and Reconstruction of Physiological Events: Acquiring the Pregnancy Identity" (paper delivered to the Annual Meeting of the Midwest Sociological Society, Chicago, Apr. 1975).

15. Rita S. Miller, "The Social Aspects of Pregnancy: A Preliminary Bibliography" (paper delivered to the Annual Meeting of the American Sociological Association, Montreal, Can., Aug. 1974).

16. *Ibid.*, pp. 41-43.

17. Alice S. Rossi, "Transition to Parenthood," *Journal of Marriage and Family*, vol. 30, no. 1 (Feb. 1968), p. 30.

18. See, for example, the discussion of graduate training by Wilbert E. Moore, *The Professions; Rules and Roles* (New York: Russell Sage Foundation, 1970).

19. See Everett C. Hughes, "Dilemmas and Contradictions of Status," *American Journal of Sociology*, vol. 50, no. 5 (Mar. 1945), pp. 353-59.

20. Ralph La Rossa, "The First Pregnancy As a Marital Crisis: What We Know and Don't Know About the Effect of the First Pregnancy on the Husband-Wife Relationship" (paper delivered to the Seventy-first Annual Meeting of the American Sociological Association, New York, Aug. 1976).

21. R. A. Rosen and Lois O. Martindale, "Contraception, Abortion and Self-Concept" (paper delivered to the Seventy-first Annual Meeting of the American Sociological Association, New York, Aug. 1976).

22. Erving Goffman, "The Moral Career of the Mental Patient," *Asylums* (Garden City, N. Y.: Doubleday, 1961), pp. 125-69.

23. Diana Scully and Pauline Bart, "A Funny Thing Happened on the Way to the Orifice: Woman in Gynecology Textbooks," *American Journal of Sociology*, vol. 78, no. 4 (Jan. 1973), pp. 1045-49.

24. Karen Paige and Jeffrey Paige, "The Politics of Birth Practices: A Strategic Analysis," *American Sociological Review*, vol. 38 (Dec. 1973), pp. 663-76.

25. Catherine Milinaire, *Birth* (New York: Harmony, 1974).

26. Irving Burstein, R. Kinch, and L. Stern, "Anxiety, Pregnancy, Labor and the Neonate," *American Journal of Obstetrics and Gynecology*, vol. 118 (1974), pp. 195-99.

27. See Fox.

28. Leonard Kovit, "Labor Is Hard Work: Notes on the Social Organization of Childbirth," *Sociological Symposium*, vol. 8 (Spring 1972), pp. 11-21.

29. W. Rosengren and S. Devault, "The Sociology of Time and Space in an Obstetrical Hospital," in E. Freidson, *et al., The Hospital in Modern Society* (New York: The Free Press, 1963), pp. 266-92.

30. Paige and Paige, pp. 663-76.

JOYCE GRIFFEN
Northern Arizona University

A Cross-Cultural Investigation of Behavioral Changes at Menopause

Two basic questions are addressed in this article: first, in what cultures are there rites of passage to move women from their reproductive years to their status as "old," and second, in what other ways is this transition eased for women in various cultures? It was hypothesized that the discipline of anthropology, which has detailed rituals performed at menarche, would also have recorded instances of rituals and their content at menopause. Further, it was hypothesized that cultures which do not provide such ceremonies will in some other way or ways indicate acceptable and unacceptable behavior during and after menopause.

Proceeding from these logical hypotheses, there are further questions. Given the presence or absence of ceremonies, what correlations exist with, for example, comparative dominance or submission of females within various cultures, or with types of descent systems, or the different activities of women within and outside the family and the household at different ages or with changed behavior of significant others in the culture vis-à-vis the menopausal woman who may be changing her roles?

Unfortunately, the cross-cultural data on menopause are so limited that the only conclusions that can be drawn are tentative at best. Because of their scarcity, these data are treated descriptively rather than statistically in this presentation. The very paucity of data suggests further explanatory hypotheses, which will be presented at the conclusion of the discussion.

The McKinlay and McKinlay "Selected Studies of the Menopause" appears to be the only recent synopsis of studies of menopause.[1] Their bibliography annotates 84 articles, fifteen of which are concerned solely with clinical trials in the area of menopausal therapy. Only three of the remaining 69 references include data from other than Caucasian women. Of the three, one is a study of 55 women in Israel "of European and Oriental origin"; another includes just over 1,300 Bantu women but reports only on an attempt to discover mean age at menopause in South Africa (Bantu women reportedly cease menstruation nine months earlier than white women in the same area); while a book published in 1897 and long out of print compares the menopausal experience of Eskimos and American Indians with that of French and Irish women.

The McKinlays pose six research questions for future investigation, two of which might profitably be investigated with reference to cross-cultural data. These are:

(1) How can the intra- and inter-societal differences in the appearance of symptoms be explained? Why is it, for example, th.;t in some societies there is no apparent evidence of "menopausal symptoms"?

(2) If the menopause signals for women the end of such socially important roles as reproducer, mother, and perhaps even wife, could it be that "menopausal" symptomatology is a manifestation of difficulties of role readjustment experienced at about this time of life?[2]

To research these questions cross-culturally, the Human Relations Area Files were used. Category 886, "Senescence," in *Outline of Cultural Materials* deals with "cultural criteria of senescence and the onset of old age, menopause (e.g., cultural interpretation, adaptive changes in behavior) . . . and retirement from active life."[3] However, 191 of the cultures indexed in the Human Relations Area Files-Microfiles collection had no entry whatsoever in the "Senescence" category, and an additional 41 had no material relevant to the hypotheses. Of the remaining approximately 35 cultures, ten noted changed behavior of both males and females in "old age." For example, both Nahane males and females restrict activities with increasing age; Burmese women are expected (as are Burmese men) to be retiring and unobtrusive in their behavior when the third age of life is reached, and in the Soviet Union management is legally obliged to release male employees at age sixty if they have completed 25 years of work or females at age 55 if they have completed 20 years of work.[4]

In eight cultures, it was specifically noted that no behavior changed for post-menopausal women. Elwin notes that "as elsewhere in aboriginal India, the climacteric does not appear to be dreaded or even especially noticed. In India, women are old at forty-five and they greet the cessation of the menstrual period with relief. . . ."[5] For the Marias, " 'As it appears, so it disappears.' If an elderly woman or her husband dreams of a dried-up tank or stream, it means that this crisis is approaching."[6] With the Lepcha, "It is realised that after a certain age women cease to conceive, but there is no break in their sexual activities."[7]

Changed behavior obviously has been recorded in only a small number of the world's cultures. One type of change noted is that of withdrawal from previous social activities. Bohannan and Bohannan noted, for example, an elderly Tiv woman who "had again 'put on the snail shell' (i.e., had declared herself no longer sexually available and had donned the insignia of this situation, usually seen only on very young girls and very old women), and had returned to live in her natal lineage with her brother."[8] The Amhara observe that "women fade more rapidly than men. As a result, the 'mabalat' or 'baltét,' a greying woman past menopause, or widow of serious mind and spirit, often takes vows as a nun. . . ."[9] More traumatically among the Rural Irish "it is commonly believed that the menopause can induce insanity; in order to ward it off, some women have retired from life in their mid-forties and, in at least three contemporary cases, have confined themselves to bed until death years later."[10]

In two other cultures, both African, menopause is reportedly viewed as a disorder, although perhaps not an unfortunate one. "A Yoruba woman is unable to accept the menopause as a natural occurrence; she rather supposes that it is a pregnancy prevented by witchcraft from terminating normally."[11] Among the Twi of Ghana, "most women, quite apart from the depressives, are worried by these social hazards of the menopause [such as the husband taking younger wives, upon whom he lavishes presents] and many of them, when they first become aware of amenorrhea, go from shrine to shrine over several years with the plaint, 'I am pregnant, but the pregnancy doesn't grow.'"[12]

There are several cultures in which behavior for post-menopausal women changes in the direction of much greater freedom. Yet, no data are recorded on women learning to operate in these heady new dimensions, or if exercise of the new privileges was sudden or gradually assumed, or if, indeed, it was not merely exercised increasingly with increasing age with no reference whatever to cessation of menses. For example, the strength of the avoidance relationship between Yap brother and sister 'diminishes markedly once the women is past menarche and when her brother is of advanced years too, and obtains only primarily during the years when both are sexually mature."[13]

Gustatory adventures await post-menopausal Thonga women. "When women have passed the time of child-bearing, most of the taboos [primarily cattle-associated taboos] cease, and they can eat monkeys and porcupine if they wish!"[14] In Tepoztlán, both old men and old women "may get drunk, insult others, use sexual terms, laugh and cry, and even urinate in public without censure, although younger people may find it embarrassing."[15] In Thailand,

men and women in this old age group [after sixty] become freer in behavior and manner. In warm weather old women often go about the house compound with their breasts uncovered even when outsiders are present. . . . The old can break many language prohibitions and speak among themselves of things that younger men and women would not mention in a mixed group.[16]

Much the same lessening of bonds is reported for the Taiwan Hokkien, of whom it is reported that "old women smoke in public, appear at public dinners normally attended by men only, and are generally outspoken."[17] These references and others seem entirely secular in tone. The Kanuri, for example, often "use old women for such purposes" as taking kola nuts as a wooing present.[18] Among the Dogon,

it is only at the moment when the woman, arriving at the threshold of old age, ceases to be a woman that she may finally feel herself truly integrated in the more stable element of the population; to observe henceforth with a critical eye the conduct of the young women whom her sons, in their turn, bring to the village, to give orders in the house, in which she will work less and less. . . .[19]

How much is such secular freedom accomplished as a result of independence from males, and what are the dimensions of acquiring such independence? Among the Kapauku, "senescence has an opposite influence on the status curve of the woman. The older she grows, the more she becomes emancipated from the powers of her husband."[20] In China "The *lao-nien* [aged—past sixty] stage was often an unusual one for women. It was often a stage in which a woman was released from male domination."[21] A final observation in this category relates to a rite among the eastern Timbira where Nimuendajú

witnessed a ceremony that publicly and formally expressed the principle that old women merit respect as much as old men. Ordinarily there is no feminine counterpart to the men's council in the plaza; but on that day [the close of the pepyé retreat in 1933] the old women were invited by the councilors to take the male elders' places in the plaza, the councilors themselves withdrawing to a spot on the margin. Then two youths and a girl hauled in a huge meat pie on a mat and handed it over to the old women, who forthwith divided it up and ate it precisely in the manner of the councilors, whereupon they went home.[22]

Finally, there are cultures in which menopause signals accession to increased social and perhaps also supernatural power.

All of these cultures, with one exception, are New World, and they are—again with only one exception—North American. The one Old World instance comes from Iran, where it is said that "making the prophet Hrezr appear is only possible for a woman who has passed the menopause."[23] Although not specifically reported to be post-menopausal, it seems obvious that the Gros Ventre women of the following quotation are just that:

Other women could join the Dance with the chief vower, but under what general conditions and procedures we did not ascertain except that to qualify either as associates or as chief vower, women had to be 'old' or 'very old,' to be 'women who had seen all of life,' and were 'beyond their prime,' not 'young women.' This would probably mean in Gros Ventre age terminology women beyond the age of about forty-five or fifty.[24]

Winnebago women could participate in construction of ceremonial lodges only if they had passed their climacterics, and after this they also could work on the buckskins of a war bundle. Attendance at feasts was possible then as well:

All the young girls nearing the age of puberty will be absent, but the old women, who have passed their climacteric, sit right next to the men, because they are considered the same as men as they have no menstrual flow any more.[25]

The same equation is made by the Northern Ojibwa, where women may exercise professional services that require supernatural license "after menopause when they are considered to be much more like men."[26]

Although not retrieved from the Human Relations Area File, three further instances belong here. The first of these relates to the Munducurú of South America, where it is reported that

all these strictures are suspended in the case of postmenopausal women. An old woman will sit where she pleases, and men will actually defer by making room for her. She may talk on whatever subject interests her, and if this requires that she interrupt the men, then so be it. Her opinions are freely given—and listened to—on matters of community concern, and they are shown marked respect. By graduating from sex and child-bearing, she has graduated from a female role and, in a legal sense, has become a man, albeit an old one.[27]

Second, Kessler noted that in Indian villages in Mexico the *curandera* "is often a woman past the menstrual cycle."[28] Finally, the Cree of western Saskatchewan have the knowledge that women cannot exercise shamanistic power until after menopause, "for women and *manito,* the force necessary to healing, are antithetical."[29]

As mentioned earlier, any attempt to draw conclusions in any way definitive from such scanty data is tentative. To begin, however, it is difficult to accept without question Kessler's assertion that "in all probability, not many women in early societies lived long enough to achieve this stage."[30] Second, and apropos of this stage of cessation, when is something "the last" (e.g., the last rainbow or the last snowfall one is to see)? "The first" is easier descriptively, if not also conceptually, and this may well hinder categorization. Clinical papers dealing with menopause, for instance, frequently resort to "no menstrual periods within the last twelve months" as a working definition.

A third possible conclusion is that most ethnographers have been male and hence barred from gathering data about the female life cycle. Fourth, perhaps all ethnographers, female as well as male, have been more oriented to youth than to old age and are thus uninterested in changes in behavior related to cessation of childbearing.

Some combination of culture area and time of investigation seems to be part of a fifth possible explanation. Are cultures which see access of females to increased power (and hence ceremonial associations, as with the making of war bundles) indeed North American almost exclusively? Or is some factor at work which made the male ethnographers working in North America more perceptive and perhaps more painstaking? And is there some correlation between the time in which these men were in the field (Radin in the Twenties and Hallowell in the Thirties) and fashions in emphasis or in training so that they recorded changed behavior in women past the menopause and other ethnographers at other times and places did not?

It would seem that the inadequate reporting may well be a combination of many of the above factors but particularly of the anti-woman, anti-aging biases within U. S. culture, the culture in which so many ethnographers have been trained. These two strikes against the gathering of data on post-menopausal behavior may be augmented by a third if the ethnographer is a female who has internalized a sexless, if not an actual anti-female, bias in order to have progressed far enough in professional training to be doing field work. For example, this author believes that without the influence of these three biases while in the field in the early Sixties, she would have been more sensitive to the behavior of three elderly women who clearly wielded power in the workings of the Southern Ute tribe.[31] Indeed, two of the three were thought to have had supernatural power. And was that power caused by or correlated with their social power? That, too, should have been investigated. Such questions would have been perceived as more legitimate, had the McKinlays only asked ten years earlier if menopausal symptoms are not indeed caused by loss of "such socially important roles as reproducer, mother, and . . . wife."[32]

Clearly the cross-cultural data available, at least as indexed in the Human

Relations Area File, are inadequate to correlate physical symptoms associated with a predictable biological phenomenon with the array of sociocultural factors found in the modern United States. Data from aboriginal North American Indian cultures strongly suggest that loss of the role of reproducer-mother-wife signals at least access to the role of curer, and that the two roles are mutually exclusive. Certainly, the hypothesis should be entertained that the magnitude of symptoms associated with menopause is positively correlated with the paucity of roles (or of availability of demeaning roles only) available to the post-menopausal woman. The Rural Irish example would seem important here.

In future research the following questions are among those which should be addressed: Why no rites of passage? Why no instruction in requisite new behavior? What must be learned, and under what conditions, to play adequately the role of "old lady"?[33] In cultures in which post-menopausal women actually gain in power, is it solely because they "have become men, albeit old ones"?

In addition to the professional challenge of seeking answers to these questions and to others which will inevitably be generated by further research, there may well be vitally important physical reasons for answering such questions. For example, without cross-cultural knowledge, women in complex industrialized nations such as the United States almost inevitably will be treated by some physicians on the basis of perceptions such as those of Wilson and Wilson. These authors published a paper entitled "The *Fate* of *Non-treated* Post-menopausal Women: A *Plea* for the Maintenance of *Adequate* Oestrogen *Therapy* from Puberty to the Grave."[34]

Scanty as are the data presented in this discussion, the author believes they make clear that no female at the approximate age of fifty suddenly faces fate. Rather, they seem to demonstrate that behavior proper to the role of elderly female is shaped by culture, as are all sex- and age-linked roles. From long before puberty the behavior of any female is a product of the interplay between her unique biological heritage, her shared sociocultural environment, and the choices she as an individual makes from among the behavioral alternatives available to her in her culture.

NOTES

1. Sonia M. McKinlay and John B. McKinlay, "Selected Studies of the Menopause," *Journal of Biosocial Science,* vol. 5, no. 4 (1973), pp. 533-55.

2. *Ibid.,* p. 537.

3. George P. Murdock *et al., Outline of Cultural Materials,* vol. 1, Behavior Science Outlines (4th rev. ed.; New Haven, Conn.: Human Relations Area Files, Inc., 1961), p. 143.

4. John Joseph Honigmann, *Culture and Ethos of Kaska Society* (New Haven: Yale University Press, 1949), p. 199; Charles S.

Brant and Mi Mi Khaing, "Burmese Kinship and the Life Cycle: An Outline," *Southwestern Journal of Anthropology,* vol. 7 (1951), p. 451; Wladyslaw Wszebór Kulski, *The Soviet Regime; Communism in Practice* (Syracuse, N. Y.: Syracuse University Press, 1954), p. 358.

5. Verrier Elwin, *The Muria and Their Ghotul* (Bombay: Oxford University Press, 1947), p. 152.

6. Wilfrid Vernon Grigson, *The Maria Gonds of Bastar* (London: Oxford University Press, 1949), p. 364.

7. John Morris, *Living with the Lepchas; A Book About the Sikkim Himalayas* (London, Toronto: W. Heinemann, 1938), p. 237.

8. Paul Bohannan and Laura Bohannan, "Three Source Notebooks in Tiv Ethnography" (manuscript; New Haven, Conn.: Human Relations Area Files, 1958), p. 268.

9. Simon David Messing, "The Highland-Plateau Amhara of Ethiopia" (Ph.D. dissertation, University of Pennsylvania, 1957), p. 481.

10. John C. Messenger, *Inis Beag, Isle of Ireland* (New York: Holt, Rinehart and Winston, 1969), p. 109.

11. P. Morton-Williams, "The Atinga Cult Among the Southwestern Yoruba: A Sociological Analysis of a Witch-Finding Movement," Institut Français d'Afrique Noire, Bulletin, Serie B, *Sciences Humaines*, vol. 18 (1956), p. 329.

12. M. J. Field, *Search for Security; An Ethno-Psychiatric Study of Rural Ghana* (New York: W. W. Norton, 1970), p. 150.

13. Edward E. Hunt, Jr., *et al.*, *The Micronesians of Yap and Their Depopulation* (Washington, D. C.: Pacific Science Board, National Research Council, 1949), p. 103.

14. Henri Alexandre Junod, *The Life of a South African Tribe* (2nd ed.; London: Macmillan, 1927), vol. 2, p. 185.

15. Oscar Lewis, *Life in a Mexican Village; Tepoztlán Restudied* (Urbana: University of Illinois Press, 1951), p. 411.

16. John E. De Young, *Village Life in Modern Thailand* (Berkeley and Los Angeles: University of California Press, 1955), p. 35.

17. Bernard Gallin and Hsin Hsing. *Taiwan: A Chinese Village in Change* (Berkeley and Los Angeles: University of California Press, 1966), p. 215.

18. Ronald Cohen, *The Kanuri of Bornu* (New York: Holt, Rinehart and Winston, 1967), p. 41.

19. Denise Paulme, *Organisation sociale des Dogon (Soudan français)* [*Social Organization of the Dogon (French Sudan)*] (Paris: Editions Domat-Montchrestien, F. Loviton et Cie., 1940), pp. 417-8.

20. Leopold J. Pospisil, *Kapauku Papuans and Their Law* (New Haven, Conn.: Yale University Press, 1958), p. 59.

21. Marion Joseph Levy, *The Family Revolution in Modern China* (Cambridge, Mass.: Harvard University Press, 1949), p. 129.

22. Curt Nimuendajú, *The Eastern Timbira*, trans. and ed. Robert H. Lowie (Berkeley and Los Angeles: University of California Press, 1946), p. 133.

23. Henri Massé, *Croyances et coutumes persanes* [*Persian Beliefs and Customs*], trans. Human Relations Area Files (2 vols.; Paris: Librairie Orientale et Americaine, 1938), p. 363.

24. John Montgomery Cooper, *The Gros Ventres of Montana: Part 2, Religion and Ritual*, ed. Regina Flannery (Washington, D. C.: Catholic University of America, 1956), p. 243.

25. Paul Radin, *The Winnebago Tribe*, U. S. Bureau of American Ethnology, Annual Report, vol. 37 (1915/1916), p. 106, p. 442, p. 137.

26. A. Irving Hallowell, *The Role of Conjuring in Saulteaux Society* (Philadelphia: University of Pennsylvania Press, 1942), p. 20.

27. Yolanda Murphy and Robert F. Murphy, *Women of the Forest* (New York and London: Columbia University Press, 1974), pp. 105-06.

28. Evelyn S. Kessler, *Women: An Anthropological View* (New York: Holt, Rinehart and Winston, 1976), p. 25.

29. Alice B. Kehoe, "The Metonymic Pole and Social Roles," *Journal of Anthropological Research*, vol. 29, no. 4 (1973), p. 270.

30. Kessler, p. 25.

31. The author completed field research with the Southern Utes from July 1 through August 15, 1962, as a research assistant for the Tri-Ethnic Research Project of the University of Colorado at Boulder. In addition, from August 15, 1962, through May 30, 1963, the author served as secretary to the director of the Southern Ute Rehabilitation Program.

32. McKinlay and McKinlay, p. 37.

33. The author is indebted to M. Jean Haviland, of the University of Southern Colorado, who suggested at the 1976 Western Social Science Association meeting in Tempe, Ariz., where this presentation was originally made, that no rite of passage and no instruction in behavior may be felt necessary. Her thought was that a woman freed of child-bearing could also now pursue her life freely and hence need not be socialized to approved behavior, a situation very different from that of the pubescent female.

34. R. A. Wilson and T. A. Wilson, "The Fate of Non-Treated Post-Menopausal Women: A Plea for the Maintenance of Adequate Oestrogen Therapy from Puberty to the Grave," *Journal of the American Geriatric Society*, vol. 11 (1963), p. 347. Words considered to be biased have been emphasized.

M. JANE SLAUGHTER
University of New Mexico

Women and Socialism: The Case of Angelica Balabanoff

Women have always played roles in the revolutionary movements of the West, and the young women in the United States in the 1960's who became involved in the radical politics of the "New Left" were not initiating a new form of activity. These same women confronted problems emerging from their involvement. They questioned whether current theoretical analyses really dealt with the causes of their own subjection, or whether their goals could ever be realized within what were male-dominated organizations. This sort of consciousness was not new either. In the last decades of the nineteenth century, as socialist parties were organized in Europe and the United States, reform-minded women joined these parties in increasing numbers.

At that time, certain of the problems resulting from women's participation in radical politics were given greater scrutiny. Socialist theory, since it dealt with women as part of the economic unit of the family, maintained that the elimination of exploitative capitalist economic relationships would automatically result in women's emancipation. The answers to questions regarding the fundamental nature of woman's reproductive role, processes of socialization, and sexual politics were only hinted at by Karl Marx, Friedrich Engels, and August Bebel.[1] There was no accepted orthodox Marxist position regarding the organization of women within the parties. Nor was there any clear consideration of the barriers which male leadership unconsciously could raise to hinder women's development.

Socialist women at the beginning of the century confronted these issues and suggested certain solutions. Since the attraction of both feminism and socialism, and the issue of the relationship between these movements (if they are indeed separate), are clearly still with us, the activities of women socialists from the beginning of the century to the close of the First World War can shed light on the contemporary search for answers and options.[2]

Using degrees of feminism as a basis for definition, there appear to have been two broad categories of women in the socialist ranks. The first group, which obviously can be described as feminist, included women such as Alexandra Kollontai, Clara Zetkin, Anna Kuliscioff, Mary White Ovington, and Dora Montefiore.[3] They dedicated their main energies to women's condition, writing tracts and essays on working women's problems, attempting to fill in theoretical gaps in socialist ideology, building separate women's organizations, and often challenging the male leadership on feminist issues.

The women of the second group are less well-known and more difficult to describe. They were sympathetic to women's problems and involved in women's organizations, but they were first and foremost socialists who did not challenge the party line or practice on feminist concerns. Angelica Balabanoff is a good representative of this group. Her background was quite similar to that of Kollontai and Kuliscioff, and she worked closely with these women. She was in an influential position as a well-known and respected leader of the international socialist movement. Nevertheless, she consistently adhered to what might be considered the traditional position of most male socialist leaders where women's issues were involved.

Comparing Balabanoff's life and actions with those of the "feminist" socialists provides a focal point for an analysis of these different positions. First, what was it that drew these women to socialism, and second, how did they respond to the theoretical and practical questions of socialism and feminism? With the exception of individuals such as the Austrian socialist Adelheid Popp,[4] the majority of "important women among the Marxist revolutionaries came from the upper classes. . . . The origin of their option for socialism and the revolution lay in a consciousness of social responsibility, indeed sympathy for the sufferings of the lower strata of the population."[5] Often through observing the position of family servants, or through an education liberally sprinkled with radical philosophy, these women chose to affiliate with socialist parties. This is not a feature unique to socialist women. The women's rights leaders in the United States in both the nineteenth century and later in the feminist activities of the 1960's were also frequently from the middle or upper class backgrounds and reacted against traditional roles assigned to women of their class. Many of them also adopted more radical positions as a result of educational experiences.[6] In this broader context, Balabanoff's girlhood and subsequent education provide a good case study.

While she was growing up on her family's estate near Kiev in the 1880's and '90's, Balabanoff showed little awareness of nineteenth century Russian radicalism or of the fact that such movements had a relatively high percentage of female participation.[7] What, then, made her turn from her family, her comfortable life, and the traditional pattern of Russian upbringing? At this point it is safe to say her consciousness was raised as a woman strongly aware of the suffering of others. Going with her mother on "charity" missions among the peasants, she saw her own privileged position and the deference with which she and her mother were treated. "I began to feel the difference between he who gives and he who must accept."[8] With this realization she began to ask annoying questions of her mother and found the answers generally unsatisfactory. A typical member of the gentry class, she was educated by tutors and sent to a fashionable girls' school in Kharkov. Her experience there proved less than stimulating: "My training was such as would fit me to my destiny—marriage to a wealthy man, a life of ease for which the conventional accomplishments and social graces were a necessary preparation. Good manners, languages, music, dancing, embroidery—these were the requisites of a Russian lady. . . ."[9] For many young women in western Europe and in the United States, similar training patterns embodied in the "cult of true womanhood" produced the same sort of reaction and discontent.

Angelica travelled with her family to Switzerland and the spas of Europe and for a time was enrolled in a language school, where she became interested in teaching. "It was the first time anyone had suggested to me a career other than idleness."[10] Upon returning home, she referred to the next two years as the "*Sturm und Drang* of my whole career." She persistently resisted her mother's matrimonial plans (a considerable feat in itself) and insisted stubbornly that she wanted to go to a university and to teach. Since it was difficult for women to gain admission to a university in Russia, her family ultimately gave in and she left Russia to attend the Université Nouvelle in Brussels. There she found another world which fascinated her. More and more she was drawn to professors who were of leftist persuasions. She flirted with anarchist ideology for a time but ultimately found the position of George Plekhanoff more appealing. He provided "a philosophy of method that gave continuity and logic to the processes of history and which endowed my own ethical aspirations with the force of dignity of an historical imperative."[11]

Gradually she began to find explanations for her own personal feelings and actions and at the same time to define more clearly what the goals and activities of her life would be. It is important to recognize that she did not interpret her own rebellion as that of a woman rejecting the standard feminine roles of the time, but rather as an individual whose humanistic spirit rejected social injustice and sought the answers for total equality through socialism. Throughout her writings Balabanoff insisted on her identification with the poor of the working class, on her sympathy for their condition, and on her desire to "break up the hated gold cage which created a barrier between them and me . . . to fulfill an obligation to repair an injustice."[12]

Balabanoff continued her education, attending the University of Leipzig and taking courses at the University of Berlin until she finally completed a degree in languages and literature. She then had to decide what she could do to help alleviate the human suffering of which she was so conscious. The answer came from her early university association with various Italian emigrés, which had created "an almost mystical bond of sympathy between me and the Italian radicals."[13] She travelled to Rome, where she applied and was accepted for membership in the Partito Socialista Italiano (PSI). Her first formal activity in the party was to work with Italian immigrant laborers in the textile mills in St. Gall, Switzerland. This work, which lasted from 1902 to 1905, carried no salary, a feature that would become characteristic of her entire life's work. Like many other young women of her time, Balabanoff had found at a relatively early age through a series of personal experiences a lifelong career and a cause to which she devoted her life.

In a comparative sense, there is no great difference between the factors which led Balabanoff to join the socialist movement and those which influenced the early course of the lives of the "feminist" socialist women. Once within the folds of socialist organizations, however, the differences in activities and attitudes among these women become more pronounced. In the areas of theoretical contribution, many women concentrated on the "woman question." In the United States, for example, by the time of the International

Socialist Meeting at Stuttgart in 1907, women such as Kate Richards O'Hare, Josephine Kaneko, and May Wood Simons had recognized that "women could not be free until they had developed the power of freedom within themselves."[14] For this reason they resisted any sort of simplified linkage of female emancipation with socialist revolution and pointed out the complex relationships between feminism and socialism.

In 1914, several issues of the *New Review* were devoted to these questions. Mary White Ovington felt feminist issues could not be dealt with strictly on class lines and stated that socialist women "will recognize that as women they have their obligation to stand with all other women who are fighting for the destruction of masculine despotism and the right of womankind."[15] Maud Thompson wrote that "Feminism . . . draws in its train, in fact, all the liberty that frees woman socially, sexually, intellectually as well as politically and economically," and Louise Kneeland concluded that "the socialist who is not a feminist lacks breadth. The feminist who is not a socialist is lacking in strategy."[16]

So, too, at this time in England, women in various socialist groups debated the relationship between feminism and socialism and insisted on the special problems women face because of their sex. Isabella Ford, who in 1904 wrote *Women and Socialism*, saw socialism and feminism as "different aspects of the same great force," while Dora Montefiore of the Social Democratic Federation, in a debate with Belfort Bax in 1909, stated that "women had a special oppression which they had to struggle against themselves."[17] In Italy in the 1890's, as the Socialist Party was developing, Anna Kuliscioff emerged as an advocate of women's rights. Her speech at a Milan study group in 1890 provided a full statement of women's condition and goals and was then looked upon as the "first realistic statement of feminism in Italy."[18] Her primary concern was with working class women, and she maintained women could never fulfill their mission in life unless they fully arrived at their own mature, individual identity.

Two other women in the same years, Alexandra Kollontai and Clara Zetkin, are clearly representative of this brand of feminist socialism. They were then, as now, well-known on an international scale for their contributions to women's emancipation. Zetkin, prior to World War I, in examining socialist theory as it related to women, "looked at women not only as economic beings, but examined sexuality as a social fact concluding that the socialist movement had to respond to the special needs of women and the oppressive conditions from which they suffered."[19] In Russia prior to the Revolution, both Bolsheviks and Mensheviks firmly opposed acknowledgement of the distinct problems of women within the working class.[20] Kollontai consistently sought to change this attitude in both her actions and essays such as the *New Morality and the Working Class* and the later *Autobiography of a Sexually Emancipated Communist Woman*, in which she attempted to deal with all facets of woman's oppression. She wrote of the need to free women from a strictly reproductive function, as well as to emancipate both men and women sexually if political and economic goals were to be fully realized. Even Inessa Armand, who was firmly in Lenin's camp in this period, was concerned throughout her life "with the woman problem in its relation to socialism," and her letters to Lenin on the subject of free love give evidence of her willingness to debate both the causes of women's oppression as well as the changes that must take place to insure true liberation.[21]

Angelica Balabanoff represents a different tradition among women socialists. Her personal statements indicate an awareness of women's particular problems. She attended the same meetings, travelled as widely, and participated in the same sort of radical activity as did Zetkin and Kollontai. Her writings are not, however, directed to women, and she does not examine or question Marxist theory or party position relative to the "woman question." In her university career, Balabanoff knew that women were not given the same opportunities or freedoms of study as were the men.[22] She was well aware that the numbers of women active in the socialist parties were relatively small and that the leaders among them were in unique positions. A great admirer of Clara Zetkin, she saw her as "the guide for an entire generation of socialist women."[23] In speaking of Rosa Luxemburg, she stated that Rosa "belonged to that generation of famous women who had to struggle against almost insurmountable obstacles to gain opportunities which the men of her day accepted as a matter of course."[24]

Later in Russia, as Balabanoff ran into difficulties in reconciling her own ethics and aspirations with those of the Bolsheviks, she reflected on her own intransigency. Her conclusion was that "women have to go through such a tremendous struggle before they are free that in their own minds that freedom is more precious to them than to men."[25] For her, the work that she and people like Zetkin did would enable "millions of working class women to move forward on the main road to socialism without losing themselves in the tortuous ways of bourgeois feminism."[26] When she and Maria Giudice founded *Su, Compagne* as a propaganda newspaper for Italian socialists, she explained her position: "Both Maria and I were hostile to any form of feminism. To us the fight for the emancipation of women was only a single aspect of the struggle for the emancipation of humanity. It was because we wanted women — particularly working class women — to understand this, to learn that they had to fight not against men, but with them against the common enemy, capitalist society . . . that this paper was founded."[27]

In her decision to follow the socialist path and to work for social equality, she did not see any contradiction between her position and rights as a woman, on the one hand, and the goals and programs of socialism, on the other. Because socialism offered "absolute social equality I never believed it necessary to dedicate myself in any special way, that is to say separately, to the questions of · antimilitarism, anticlericalism, or to that of the emancipation of women."[28] With the aid of hindsight, one might conclude that the position of Balabanoff (and others like her) was naive and lacking precise analysis. However, "her idea of socialism had always been practical and direct. Philosophy and theory, for her, meant a kind of egalitarian ethic, a quasi-religious socialism which exalted the poor and downtrodden and demanded they be granted full human stature."[29] In her eyes, concentration on the problems of any single group in society would have been hypocritical.

Where practical activities are concerned, the divergencies between the two types of women socialists are better seen as the differences between leaders and followers. Two issues, the question of separate organizations for women and of women's suffrage, illustrate the practical activity related to feminist concerns. Marxist theory was clearly ambiguous on the issue of organizing women, for in 1868 Marx himself had favored "the formation of women's branches" or "female branches of the working class without however interfering with the existing formation of branches composed of both sexes."[30] At a later time, Lenin indicated that there should be "no special organization for women. A woman communist is a member of the party just as a man communist with equal rights and duties." Nevertheless, he also supported appropriate bodies to carry on the work among backward peasant women, but "that is not feminism, that is practical revolutionary expediency."[31]

In the midst of such inconsistency, the activist women already referred to worked hard in the period prior to World War I to build women's groups. In the United States in 1908, the Party formally recognized a Woman's Committee with May Wood Simons as Chair. Women delegates at the party convention of that year also won party endorsement of the equal suffrage plank. On the British socialist scene, regardless of male opposition, women's organizations, such as the Women's Labour League of the Independent Labour Party, were created and encouraged women's suffrage with a variety of arguments. Dora Montefiore, for example, was a member of one of the women's circles of the Social Democrat Federation and also a member of the Women's Social Political Union.[32] In Italy, Kuliscioff organized women in the PSI as the Union of Women Socialists. By 1916, there were seventy sections of the Union, and the Party officially recognized their existence and the right to draw funds directly from the secretary's office.[33]

The women's Union concentrated on regulation of working conditions for women but also supported suffrage. In party meetings in 1908 and 1910, Kuliscioff introduced resolutions advocating women's right to vote, but it was not until the 1911 meeting at Modena that such a resolution was accepted.[34] It was largely through Zetkin's effort that at the 1907 Stuttgart congress women's suffrage was introduced as a party issue. At her instigation, an International Women's Secretariat was founded and planning begun for International Women's Congresses. Meetings were held at Copenhagen in 1910 and 1913, and a major conference was set for March 26-28, 1915, in Berne.[35] During the Russian Revolution, Zetkin was involved in Working Women's Conferences and served as president of the secretariat of the International Conference of Women held in 1920.

Kollontai's activities, though confined primarily to work within Russia, closely resembled those of Zetkin. Between 1908 and 1921, Kollontai spent considerable energy in the organization of working class women, and, though from time to time under party pressure she gave up this work, she was instrumental in the formation and operation of a Women's Bureau and in gaining the recognition by the Ninth Congress of the Russian Communist Party of the existence of women's sections.[36] Clearly, the majority of the women who spoke and wrote on the theoretical aspects of feminism's relation to socialism were also in the forefront of activities designed to further the organization of women and to bring about female emancipation.

But what of the other group of women like Balabanoff who did not challenge or examine party policy relating to women? What was their involvement in activities already mentioned? Though they did not originate plans and programs for women's organizations or insist on such programs in the face of opposition from party leadership, they did support the activities of women like Kuliscioff and Zetkin. For example, when Balabanoff first worked for the PSI in Switzerland, her rooms were a meeting place for women. There she shared everything with them, including her clothing, a means she considered appropriate to liberating herself from the external vestiges of her bourgeois origins. She also spoke up strongly against the claimed exploitation of young women living in boarding houses run by the Catholic Church. When Kuliscioff began to organize women socialists in Italy, Balabanoff served as a section leader and on the Executive Committee of the Union.[37] On an international level, she represented Italy at the woman's meetings which Zetkin sponsored, and she helped in planning the International Women's Conference at Berne.[38] In Russia during the Revolution, Balabanoff always was concerned with the living and working conditions of peasant women and attended meetings of the Women's Conference, but her official posts where those of Commissar of Foreign Affairs in Kiev and, for a time, Secretary of the International.

By 1920, when Balabanoff had decided she must leave Russia, she also broke with Zetkin, of whom she said, "I realized I could no longer look to her either as a friend or as a teacher."[39] The cause of the break had nothing to do with feminist issues. Instead she saw Zetkin as a tool of Zinoviev, a man whose methods she detested. "I was not naive enough to think I could fight these methods without resorting myself to identical means. . . . I knew I was quite incapable of functioning on such a level. . . . Only by leaving Russia could I recover my socialist activity."[40] Though Balabanoff did not break with the revolutionary socialist leadership on any feminist issue, she did so when she felt her personal absolutism and her idealistic and emotional devotion to the alleviation of human misery were compromised. As her obituary in *Corriere della Sera* pointed out, "The only monogamy to which she felt morally pledged was to that of her ideology."[41]

In order to present as clear a picture as possible of the activities of the women under discussion one final factor must be mentioned. When crucial international controversies arose, all of these women, with rare exception, put their feminist concerns aside. Thus, with the outbreak of the First World War, the conflict between resolutions for peace and neutrality versus nationalist goals occupied socialist energies. The solidarity of the international socialist women's movement was disrupted as individual women either began to organize international peace movements (as Balabanoff did) or chose to support their nation's position.[42] So, too, the outbreak of the Russian Revolution and debates within socialist parties over whether they would support and join the Third International overshadowed demands for women's emancipation. This pattern continued in the Twenties and Thirties as feminism within socialism was greatly diluted. "In the context of hunger marches, Spain and anti-fascism, young women who inclined towards radicalism had more pressing political choices. They were likely to be dismissive of feminism."[43] Given the strongly humanistic base of much of their concern and perhaps unconscious patterns of socialization which defined femininity in terms of self-sacrifice, no doubt many women felt emphasis on the issues of their own sex would be selfish.

Examining the activities and attitudes of women in the socialist parties at the beginning of this century makes it clear that contemporary debates resulting from women's involvement in radical politics are not new in history. This tie with the past provides some lessons. Though the sensitivity and support of women like Balabanoff provide a base from which women can work toward self-actualization, without the Kollontais and Zetkins asserting a feminist perspective in the scope of revolutionary activity, it is probable that many of the barriers to emancipation could not be challenged and surmounted. In the spirit of Kuliscioff and Zetkin, it is clear that regardless of the breadth of revolutionary goals and programs, these cannot be fulfilled unless women organize themselves with the purpose of arriving at a mature self-confidence and identity through which they can reconcile the "experiences of their personal lives and their commitment to political struggles."[44]

NOTES

1. In addition to the original works of these individuals, consult Hal Draper, "Marx and Engels on Women's Liberation," *International Socialism* (July-Aug. 1970), and Muriel Schein and Carol Lopate, "On Engels and the Liberation of Women," *Liberation*, vol. 16, no. 9 (Feb. 1972).

2. Contemporary essays by Juliet Mitchell and Sheila Rowbotham, as well as articles, such as that by Renate Bridenthal, "The Dialectics of Production and Reproduction in History," *Radical America*, vol. 10, no. 2 (Mar.-Apr. 1976), illustrate this point.

3. The label "feminist" would clearly have been rejected by all these women, as to them it meant one who consciously rejected the materialist analysis of women's oppression. See Mary Alice Waters, "Feminism and the Marxist Movement," *International Socialist Review* (Oct. 1972), p. 19.

4. For a good discussion of Popp, see Ingrun Lafleur, "Adelheid Popp and Working-Class Feminism in Austria," *Frontiers*, vol. 1, no. 1 (Fall 1975).

5. Alexandra Kollontai, *The Autobiogra-*

phy of a Sexually Emancipated Communist Woman (New York: Schocken Books, 1975), p. 107.

6. For comparative purposes, consider the lives of Margaret Fuller, the Grimké sisters, and Charlotte Perkins Gilman. Also see Jo Freeman, "Origins of the Woman's Movement," in *Changing Women in a Changing Society*, ed. Joan Huber (Chicago: University of Chicago Press, 1973), and Karen Sacks, "The Class Roots of Feminism," *Monthly Review*, vol. 27, no. 9 (Feb. 1976).

7. A good general statement on the Russian women can be found in Robert H. McNeal, "Women in the Russian Radical Movement," *Journal of Social History*, vol. 5 (1971-72).

8. Alessandro Schiavi (ed.), *I buoni artieri*, Part I (Rome: Opere Nuove, 1957), p. 9.

9. Angelica Balabanoff, *My Life As a Rebel* (New York: Greenwood Press, 1968), p. 17.

10. *Ibid.*, p. 22.

11. *Ibid.*, pp. 26, 32.

12. Schiavi, p. 28.

13. Balabanoff, *My Life As a Rebel*, p. 27.

14. Mari Jo Buhle, "Women and the Social-

ist Party, 1901-1914," *Radical America,* vol. 4, no. 2 (Feb. 1970), p. 40.

15. Mary White Ovington, "Socialism and the Feminist Movement," *The New Review,* vol. 2, no. 3 (Mar. 1914), p. 147.

16. *The New Review,* vol. 2, no. 8 (Aug. 1914), pp. 447, 442.

17. Sheila Rowbotham, *Hidden from History* (New York: Random House, 1974), pp. 93, 97.

18. Anna Kul\iscioff, *I memoria* (Milan: Lazarri, 1926), pp. 213-54, 154; Alessandro Schiavi, *I pionieri del socialismo in Italia: Anna Kuliscioff* (Rome: Opere Nuove, 1955), p. 79.

19. Lafleur, "Adelheid Popp," p. 87. See also Clara Zetkin, *Lenin on the Woman Question and Reminiscences of Lenin* (New York: International Publisher, 1934).

20. Anne Bobroff, "The Bolsheviks and Working Women, 1905-1920," *Radical America,* vol. 10, no. 3 (May-June 1976), p. 52.

21. Bertram Wolfe, "Lenin and Inessa Armand," personal copy of article published in *Slavic Review,* vol. 22 (Mar. 1963), p. 100, and *The Woman Question* (New York: International Publisher, 1951), pp. 76-80.

22. Balabanoff, *My Life As a Rebel,* p. 34.

23. Schiavi, *I buoni artieri,* pp. 17-18.

24. Balabanoff, *My Life As a Rebel,* p. 36.

25. Louise Bryant, *Mirrors of Moscow* (New York: Thomas Seltzer, 1923), p. 169.

26. Angelica Balabanoff, *Ricordi di una socialista* (Rome: Donatello di Luigi, 1946), p. 83.

27. Balabanoff, *My Life As a Rebel,* p. 49.

28. Balabanoff, *Ricordi,* p. 49.

29. Ronald Florence, *Marx's Daughters* (New York: Dial Press, 1975), p. 177.

30. Draper, "Marx and Engels," p. 27.

31. Zetkin, *Lenin on the Woman Question,* p. 15 and V. I. Lenin, "L'emancipazione della donna," *L'Ordine Nuovo,* vol. 2, no. 34 (Jan 1920), p. 98.

32. Rowbotham, p. 97.

33. Franca Pieroni Bortolotti, "Femminismo e socialismo dal 1900 al primo dopoguerra," *Critica Storica,* Jan. 31, 1969, p. 51.

34. Kul-iscioff, pp. 41, 310-12, 325. Also see Bortolotti, "Femminismo e socialismo," p. 40, and Nadia Spano and Fiamma Camarlinghi, *La questione femminile nella politica del PCI, 1921-1963* (Rome: Editore Donne Politica, 1972), p. 101, fn. 2.

35. For more detail on this meeting see Balabanoff's works as well as Lafleur, pp. 88, 91-92; Alfred E. Senn, *The Russian Revolution in Switzerland, 1914-17* (Madison: University of Wisconsin Press, 1971), p. 41; and Aurelia Camparini, "Il movimento femminile nei primi anni della Internazionale Comunista, 1919-1921," *Movimento Operaio e Socialista,* vol. 20, no. 1 (Jan.-Mar. 1974).

36. Bobroff, "The Bolsheviks and Working Women," p. 67. Louise Bryant and Jacques Sadoul, *Quarante lettres de Jacques Sadoul* (Paris: n.p., 1922) give good "outside" commentary on Kollontai's work.

37. Partito Socialista Italiano, *Sessant'anni di socialismo a Milano* (Milan: Avanti!, 1952), p. 24, and Spano and Camarlinghi, *La questione femminile,* p. 101.

38. Balabanoff, *My Life As a Rebel,* p. 148, and *Ricordi,* pp. 84-85.

39. Balabanoff, *My Life As a Rebel,* p. 317.

40. *Ibid.,* p. 261, and *Ricordi,* p. 333.

41. *Corriere della Sera,* Nov. 26, 1965, p. 3.

42. For her activities in this area, see *Seconde Conference Socialiste Internationale de Zimmerwald,* Kienthal, Apr. 1916, pp. 24-30 (photostat of original proceedings at the New York Public Library), and Horst Lademacher (ed.), *Die Zimmerwalder Bewegung: Protokalle und Korrespondenz* (2 vols.; Paris: Editor Mouton, 1967).

43. Rowbotham, p. 163.

44. Lafleur, "Adelheid Popp," p. 99.

SYLVIA GONZALES
San Jose State University

The White Feminist Movement:
The Chicana Perspective

In the last days of June of 1975, a historical precedent was set. Women from all over the world met in Mexico City at the International Women's Year Conference to discuss their universal state of oppression. Chicana enthusiasm for this event, marked by years of struggle toward recognition on an equal level with men, could only be matched by a sense of defeat in the realization that no Chicanas were officially or unofficially recognized at this historical meeting. Once again history repeated itself in the name of international sisterhood.

Although history has testified to oppression and discrimination since the Garden of Eden, when one sex represented good and the other evil, never before had an oppressed majority gathered together on an international scale to discuss their plight. But then, no other oppression has extended beyond physical boundaries, beyond race, color and religious beliefs, beyond economic and class differences. Only the discrimination against and the oppression of women has managed to achieve these limits. Thus, in challenging female oppression, humankind will have to travel to the very core of oppression, man versus woman. As Brownmiller has so eloquently documented in *Against Our Will*, women will have to confront the reality of every woman's rape if this oppression and discrimination is ever to be overcome.[1]

The human species has been physically endowed to preserve and persevere. Yet mankind has sought to present the act of procreation as symbolic testimony to superior and inferior status. And until this first attack on womankind is challenged, mankind will continue in more sophisticated ways to insure his legacy of superiority over future generations.

The meeting in Mexico City was both exciting and frightening from the above perspective. Could it be that humankind was finally striving to end this oppression and discrimination by challenging its most primitive and universal form? Would this challenge signal the final stage in ending the cycle of discrimination and oppression? Was the last bulwark of inhumanity and injustice finally being confronted? Was the meeting in Mexico City successful? Did substance finally predominate or was the meeting just another example of token acquiescence to oppression?

This meeting, and feminism in general, have provoked a shocking reassessment of male superiority. Men have been forced to consider their superiority as simply an illusion of their own creation supported by demonstrations of greater physical prowess. In their conflict, they sway back and forth between true attempts at sensitivity and violent withdrawals into masculinity.

Their dilemma is not easily resolved. Men have been conditioned into behavioral patterns for thousands of years. Theirs has been the role of leader and changer of society's goals, the mental and physical strength of nations. They have been reared to assume this position unquestioningly. These patterns of behavior are not easily changed.

At the same time, women have also been conditioned into certain roles. They have been witnesses of and active participants in history. Just as mankind has acted and taught oppression, women have incorporated and internalized into their image the concept of being logical objects of oppression. For women, the questions are whether they can escape the image of oppression, whether they can overcome these role definitions which have heretofore been an integral part of their learning experience, and finally, whether they can achieve positions of power and authority.

THE HIERARCHY OF OPPRESSION

One can attempt to analyze oppression in the United States by seeing it as a hierarchy of power where the white male commands at the top. Minorities have perceived this hierarchy of oppression as following an order of white male, white female, minority male, and finally, minority female. It has often been disputed whether the white female or the minority male follows in this hierarchy. During the early years of the civil rights movement, white women found a natural ally in minority males. White women turned to partnership with the minority male and his cause in naive protest to the oppressive forces of society, while remaining oblivious to her own oppression. This diversionary act by the white female to her own oppression forced her into an unnaturally patronizing posture toward minority males, who then accused white women of castration. The white male viewed this alliance between white female and minority male as an act of revolt. They also accused white females of castration because of their attempts at hierarchical influence. A vivid description of the politics of white female-black male interaction during the early years of the civil rights movement is contained in *Meridian*, a novel by black writer Alice Walker.[2]

The minority male saw union with the white female as both a blow to his white male oppressor and a calling card into this oppressor's hierarchy of power. He chose to align himself with the white female for the sake of societal expression and upward mobility. The minority male bore the brunt of white male oppression/white female castration and for psychological survival turned his oppressive needs on the minority female. This put the minority female on the bottom rung of the power ladder. Oppression by her male counterpart has alienated the minority woman from his cause since white feminism often represents the white woman's earlier partnership with the minority male and the rejection and disregard of the minority female by both the minority male and white female.

The one factor that has broken this vicious cycle of oppressive power, by defining discrimination in sexist as well as racist terms, has been the feminist movement. A new awareness of herself and her own needs helped the white female recognize that men need not be the sole instrument or object of her expression. She was then able to abandon her patronizing partnership with the minority male. Feminists are now acknowledging careers and support systems with other women as adequate defenses for withstanding the oppressive forces of male society. This example of the white female has assisted the Chicana in identifying her problem as not only an oppressed minority within Anglo society, but as an oppressed minority within the Chicano subculture.

As long as each of these groups continue in their pursuit of hierarchal power, the oppressive forces in this country are strengthened, and indisputedly, ethnic minority women continue to be at the bottom of the hierarchy. In the United States, Anglo feminists have taken the lead in the struggle for equalization of the sexes. There can be no doubt that it was white women who set this humanitarian revolution in motion. The Chicana must now utilize this movement and develop it to her advantage, for she, along with other ethnic minority women, has borne the weight of greater discriminatory practices.

SOURCES OF CHICANA OPPRESSION

First of all, Chicanas suffer as a minority in society. Because Chicanas are part of an oppressed nationality, they are subjected to the racism practiced against Chicanos. This racism accompanies the fact that the overwhelming majority of Chicanos are workers. Therefore, Chicanas are also victims of any exploitation of the working class. This cause and effect relationship immediately levels two forms of discrimination at the Chicana. This is compounded by the fact that Chicanas suffer as women within the context of the Chicano movement itself. In part, the awakening of Chicana consciousness has been prompted by the "machismo" she has encountered in the movement.

In the realm of folklore and literature, the Chicana is perceived as a woman whose passive, emotional, and masochistic nature have made her the perfect partner of the "macho" to treat or mistreat as he pleases.[3] Popular Mexican ballads such as "Juan Charrasqueado" pay tribute to poor "*Juan Ranchero, enamorado, borracho y jugador que a las mujeres mas bonitas se llevaba, de aquellos campos no quedaba ni una flor.*"[4] Translated literally, "Johnny Cowboy is a drunk, a lover, and a playboy who steals all the beautiful women until there is not a 'flower' left in the fields." And the songs continue as in "Feria de las Flores," where supposedly another Juan Ranchero takes all the "flowers" and "transplants" them in his garden. If the Chicana is not a flower to be planted and transplanted at will in the male's garden, then she is "*una ingrata*" (an ingrate) or "*traicionera*" (a traitor).

Because of these negative perceptions of the Chicana as having no control over her destiny, her input into the direction of the Chicano movement has been almost nonexistent. This image of the Chicana has given the impression within her own community that she has nothing of substance to contribute to decision-making. Although some token inclusion on local boards and community agencies has taken place within the last five years, Chicanas are still largely under-represented in policy-making positions in both public and private organizations. When opportunities do arise, Chicanos are quick to declare that such positions should go first to a Chicano male. Later, when discrimination has been defeated for him, then he will see to the Chicanas. In those few instances where a Chicana does attain an administrative position, she is often ignored by her Chicano contemporaries and made to feel like a nonentity. This is a defensive mechanism employed by Chicanos to relieve them of their own insecurity.

For the professional Chicana, the implications of this are unique. As Octavio Paz has described in "Sons of Malinche," Mexican men have conflicting images of women as either virgins or mother figures, epitomized by the Virgin of Guadalupe, or as prostitutes or traitors, represented by La Malinche.[5] Neither image offers the authority role which supposedly only men are capable of commanding. This conflict poses a singular situation for the Chicano male caught between two cultures and two value systems in that it is more difficult to explain or understand the origins of his feelings. The Chicano has learned to associate feminine qualities with the mother role. Intellectualism or professionalism are considered masculine characteristics. If the Chicana possesses feminine qualities while at the same time occupying a professional position, Chicanos experience conflict in recognizing mother-like characteristics outside the mother role. His instinct tells him that women do not belong in these positions, but his confusion is how to attack this woman who possesses the qualities of the sacred mother. If, on the one hand, the Chicana assumes an aggressive or a nonmaternal posture, his reaction to her is more clearly defined. In the first instance, the Chicano seeks ways to disgrace or challenge that image in order to reconcile the conflict. In the second instance, the Chicano simply finds fault with the Chicana's professional capabilities.

Thus, although Chicanas have played an equally significant role in shaping the Mexican American experience, traditionally they have been relegated to a substandard position. Chicanas have been ignored, their accomplishments have gone unrecognized, and their needs have been neglected. The Chicana's role has been rigidly defined as passive. It seems as if they have been invisible. Yet even today, there are activist Chicanas who engage themselves in the polemics of the validity of Octavio Paz and, falling into the trap of what he has identified as "the great lie," refuse to confront this serious deficiency in the Chicano movement and attack it at its source. The Chicano male must realize that he cannot achieve true liberation while being unwilling to share his revolution with the Chicana. Together they must free themselves from their mutual oppression and, most important, free the Chicana from Chicano oppression.

There is no doubt that the Chicano male is guilty of a crime against Chicanas when he seeks to use and then suppress them. The question is, should the Chicana seek support from the Anglo feminist movement in order to establish her role within the Chicano movement? The potential for conflict

coming out of such a decision-making process is overwhelming. One must re-
member that the origins of the Anglo feminist movement are within a society
that has transmitted through its many institutions oppressive attitudes toward
minorities. Since the male traditionally bears the brunt of this offense to his
personal pride and dignity because of greater social interaction, his home has
become the target for his misguided value as a human being or for his reactionary machismo. Chicanas do not deny that machismo is a trait deeply
rooted in the historical past of the Mexican, but it has been exaggerated
within the hostile and oppressive environment in which the Chicano finds
himself in this country. While Chicanas do not want to sacrifice themselves as
the instrument of compromise between Chicanos and the dominant society,
they must in turn ask themselves if they can become free from the Chicano's
anger and frustration through the Anglo feminist movement, a segment of
that very society which has been the origin of so much of their oppression.

Chicanas must not jump from their own oppression into that of white
women without first reaching an understanding of themselves and their
unique needs, and without demanding Chicano participation in this understanding. If they do, they will once again find themselves the peons of a strict
patronage system imposed on them, this time by the white female. But if this
understanding is reached with the Chicano, then both racism and oppression
of the Chicana could be confronted and challenged.

This is not to say that Chicanas should not reach an understanding with
the feminist movement. Many Chicanas are calling for an understanding by
and from both Anglo and Chicana feminists. Chicanas realize that if it had
not been for the white feminist movement, attention would not have been
given to the inferior status of the Chicana. The Anglo feminist movement has
also served as an awakening for the Chicana to her own condition. As Sutherland, in *Sisterhood is Powerful,* writes, "although Chicana resistance to
women's liberation is understandable, she should be able to realize that the
struggle for the liberation of her people is directly linked with her own liberation as a woman."[6] But Chicanas must ask, where is the white woman's understanding? Do white feminists recognize that if they assume an equal position
now with third world women, they can in the future conquer male and class
oppression on all fronts?

The International Women's Conference in Mexico City was indicative of
the Chicana's position within the Anglo feminist movement. Chicanas initiated a campaign to insure their representation in Mexico City. Community
groups of activist Chicanas held food fairs, car washes, dances, etc., to
finance travel to the conference. But Chicana enthusiasm was quashed by the
revelation that the sorrowful position Chicanas occupy within the feminist
movement in the United States was to be repeated in Mexico City.

The Anglo woman found herself in the same ironical contradiction as the
Chicano male as she approached the Mexico City conference. She was asked
to leave racial prejudices behind in pursuit of true international sisterhood.
But past experiences within the United States offered little in the way of guidance for this task. Claims of breaking the bonds of prejudice by including a

black perspective in the movement are left wanting in light of the continued serious neglect of ethnic minority women such as Chicanas, Puerto Ricans, Asians, and American Indians. This patronization emanates from a lopsided East Coast perspective, where black women are the largest minority and have greater visibility than other minority women. Black women must pay attention to this. In this case, black women are not oppressors by intent, but because they are less linguistically distinct, communication is more easily established. In addition, the national moral conscience is black-influenced and permeates the eastern liberal mentality to the point where liberal program responses are mainly directed to the black cause. The question put to black women from the above argument is whether they have also fallen victim to the oppressor's image, and what is their responsibility in bringing other ethnic women into their ranks.

Yet, even in the case of black women, when any minority woman is included in feminist activities, commissions, clubs, or organizations, it is usually under the title of committee or subcommittee on minority women and rarely as president or chairwoman. Before and after Mexico City, there have been numerous conferences and workshops held throughout the nation to discuss the issues. Planning committees and program announcements testify to panels on minority women as sub topics and under lengthy lists of Anglo women organizers.

THE CHICANA IN FACT AND FICTION

What is the resolution to this situation? First of all, the Chicana stereotype must be challenged. A review of existing research reveals a lack of data and a distorted and inaccurate image of the Chicana. The small body of knowledge that does exist on the Chicano has been collected mainly by Anglos, who have lacked sufficient understanding and sensitivity to the total culture of Mexicans living in the United States.

This research has dysfunctional consequences for the Chicano because of the perpetuation of false and stereotypical images of the role and function of women within the Chicano community. In large measure, these unfortunate products emanate from the activities of Anglo social institutions which, lacking counter-images of the Chicana, tend towards unquestioning acceptance of prevailing myths. For instance, educational, health, welfare and law enforcement institutions utilize these distorted pictures in developing programs to respond to needs of Chicanas. By relying on these incorrect stereotypes, these institutions and related service organizations inevitably are misguided and misinformed. Based on this misinformation, their program approach has forced Chicanas to assume the unnatural position of passivity and subservience expected of them. This has effectively barred them from a full and creative role in society.

An influential and typical example of a respected book which has contributed to the perpetuation of false and negative stereotypes of the Chicana is William Madsen's anthropological work, *Mexican Americans of South Texas,* which portrays the Chicana as weak, submissive and overly respective towards her husband and male-dominated society in general. He writes that ". . . the Mexican American wife who irritates her husband may be beaten . . . . Some wives assert that they are grateful for punishment at the hands of their husbands for such concern with shortcomings indicates profound love."[7] This study, used in many colleges and universities as an authoritative source, advances a number of totally erroneous conceptions about Chicanas. Unfortunately, this is but one, very typical, source book.

In addition to scholarly writings on Chicanas, it should be recognized that the fictional literature of any society performs an important role in shaping the mores, values, and even hostilities and anxieties of the culture. American literature on Mexican themes has always been alien and often hostile to the original settlers of the American Southwest. These attitudes can be traced to some of the most notable historical accounts of the Southwest, which present the Chicana as a fallen woman and a partner of the evil *"bandido."*[8] These stereotypes have in turn been accentuated by the media, which to date generally present the Chicana and her culture in a negative context. Descriptions of the role and image of the Chicana in American life require that if any useful and accurate contributions to scholarly research or the media are to be expected in the future, they must be made by or with the assistance of Chicanas.

In the realm of the social sciences and literature, then, the Chicana is perceived as a woman whose passive, emotional, and lazy nature has made her view her subjugation to the macho not only justifiable, but desirable. Because of these negative perceptions of the Chicana as a nonthinking being, her input into the professions has been almost nonexistent. Hence, it follows that in her own community she is also viewed as having nothing to contribute. Clearly, the next result this slanted image of the Chicana in Anglo American culture produces is the exclusion of Chicanas from all facets and levels of decision-making. This is one area where statistics are not lacking. Chicanas are drastically under-represented in policy-making positions in public and private institutions. This situation is especially acute in politics, governmental agencies, and all levels of the educational system.

It is as misleading to say that all women are alike as it is to imagine that all minorities are alike. There are characteristics and experiences unique to Chicanas that demand sharper focus than has been provided by national women's organizations. Chicanas, as is true of other minority women, are doubly discriminated against as members of an ethnic-cultural minority and as women. Chicanas are also cast into the position of being a minority within the ranks of Anglo American women.

Chicanas share with other women a concern for achieving constitutionally mandated rights in all spheres of society. However, on issues relating to Chicanas as members of a total community, there is necessarily a divergence from the broad path of national organizations of women in general. The very existence of Chicana organizations is an indicator of attempts by Chicanas to attract attention to issues that affect them. Chicana conferences are another indicator of efforts to coalesce and examine their position vis-à-vis each other,

the men in their communities, and other women's groups. The National Chicana Conference, held in Houston, Texas, in May 1971, indicated the vast
spectrum of viewpoints held by Chicanas. More than 600 Chicanas attended.
The resolutions of the two largest workshops, "Sex and the Chicana" and
"Marriage Chicana Style," called for "free, legal abortions and birth control
for the Chicano community, controlled by Chicanas." The resolution stated
that "as Chicanas, we have a right to control our own bodies." The resolutions
also called for 24-hour child care centers in Chicano communities and explained that there is a critical need for these, since "Chicana motherhood
should not preclude educational, political, social and economic advancement."[9]

While these resolutions articulated the most pressing needs of Chicanas
today, the conference as a whole reflected a rising consciousness of the Chicana of her special oppression in society. It also indicated a growing align-
ment with the goals of the Anglo women's feminist movement in this country.

In her article, "Women: New Voice of La Raza," Mirta Vidal has clearly
indicated the mutual needs and goals of both Anglo and Chicana women.[10]
The opinions expressed by Ms. Vidal in this publication reflect those of many
Chicanas throughout the country. They deal not only with the special needs
of Chicanas, but propose that Chicanas align themselves with the Anglo
Women's Liberation Movement because the struggle of all women is the
same:

With their growing involvement in the struggle for Chicano liberation and emergence
of the feminist movement, Chicanas are beginning to challenge every social institution
which contributes to and is responsible for their oppression, from inequality on the
job to their role in the home. They are questioning 'machismo,' discrimination in education, the double standard, the role of the Catholic Church, and all the backward
ideology designed to keep women subjugated.[11]

Linda Peralta Aguilar in her article, "Unequal Opportunity and the Chicana," feels that the threat to machismo in the home has had severe consequences for the Chicana on the job. Because the situation in the home has
changed somewhat, a transference is made to professional interaction. Chicanos, by depriving their women of decent wages, deprive themselves of a
good future. By depriving their women, they deprive their children and thus
their future.[12]

Vidal's chief argument is that because sexism and male chauvinism are so
deeply rooted in this society, there is a strong tendency, even within the Chicano movement, to deny the basic right of Chicanas to organize around their
own concrete issues. Instead, they are told to stay away from the women's
feminist movement because it is an "anglo thing." Women need only to
analyze the origin of male supremacy to expose this false position.

Among the many distortions about the feminist movement listed by Vidal
is the argument that women are simply fighting against men. Thus, since the
feminist movement is considered anti-male, Chicanas attempting to organize
against their own oppression are accused of trying to divide the Chicano
movement. While it is true that unity for *La Raza* is the basic foundation of

the Chicano movement, an appeal for unity based on the continued submission of women is a false one. When Chicano men talk about maintaining *"la familia"* and the cultural heritage of *La Raza,* they are in fact talking about maintaining the age-old concept of keeping the woman barefoot, pregnant, and in the kitchen. On the basis of the subordination of women, there can be no real unity. The only real unity between men and women is the unity forged in the course of struggle against their oppression. Therefore, by supporting rather than opposing the struggles of women, Chicanos and Chicanas can genuinely unite. Stripped of all rationalizations, when Chicanos deny support to the independent organization of Chicanas, they are simply saying that Chicanos are not oppressed.

CONCLUSION

There is no one Chicana perspective, but instead several different facets that have not yet become complemented so that Chicanas of varying persuasions can cooperate at a faster pace than they can pull apart. Chicanas have learned much since the Houston Conference of 1971 about the underlying processes that hinder their development and, by extension, that of Chicano communities.

Primary among these is the need for the Anglo feminist to become more sensitive to Chicana needs and aid in her struggle. The most reasonable vehicle for accomplishing this is through the incorporation of the Chicana perspective in all courses included in Women's Studies. Women's Studies departments throughout the country must take the leadership in demanding greater research in this area. They must seek the assistance of Chicana faculty and community women in their program planning. A course on the Chicana should be included as a regular curriculum offering rather than just an insignificant reference when discussing minority women. A library and research center on the Chicana should be encouraged by supporters of Women's Studies.

With the new unity demonstrated by Hispanic women at the national conference sponsored by the Women's Research Program of the National Institute of Education in June of 1976, course content could include the three major Hispanic groups — the Chicanas, Puerto Ricans, and Cubanas. Hispanics now number twenty million nationally. With the projected birth rate, they will outnumber the black population of this country within an estimated five years.[13] Women's Studies must be prepared to respond to the educational needs of this increasing group.

NOTES

1. Susan Brownmiller, *Against Our Will* (New York: Simon and Schuster, 1975), pp. 11-15.

2. Alice Walker, *Meridian* (New York: Harcourt, Brace and Jovanovich, 1976).

3. See William Madsen, *North from Mexico* (Boston: Little, Brown and Co., 1968); Celia Heller, *Mexican American Youth; Youth Forgotten At the Crossroads* (New York: Random House, 1966); Margaret Clark, *Health in the*

Mexican American Culture (Berkeley: University of California Press, 1959).

4. Francisco Xavier Aceves, *Canciones Folkloricas Mexicanas* (Guadalajara: Private Press, n.d.).

5. Octavio Paz, *Labyrinth of Solitude* (New York: Grove Press, 1961).

6. Elizabeth Sutherland, "Colonized Women, The Chicana," in *Sisterhood Is Powerful*, ed. Robin Morgan (New York: Vintage Press, 1970), pp. 376-79.

7. William Madsen, *The Mexican Americans of South Texas* (New York: Holt, Rinehart and Winston, 1973), pp. 35-36.

8. Ralph P. Bieber (ed.), *The Southwest Historical Series*, vol. 6 (Glendale, Calif.: Arthur H. Clark Co., 1938), p. 238.

9. Cecilia Suarez, The National Chicana Foundation, *Chicana Research Proposal* (Los Angeles: UCLA Chicano Studies, 1972).

10. Mirtal Vidal, "Women: New Voices of La Raza," *Chicanas Speak Out* (New York: Pathfinder Press, 1971), pp. 3-15.

11. *Ibid.*

12. Linda Aguilar, "Unequal Opportunity and the Chicana," *Civil Rights Digest*, vol. 5, no. 4 (Spring 1973), pp. 31-33.

13. *San Antonio Express*, Apr. 19, 1976, p. 15-A.

HERBERT M. KRITZER
Rice University

THOMAS M. UHLMAN
University of Missouri-St. Louis

Sisterhood in the Courtroom: Sex of Judge and Defendant in Criminal Case Disposition

One aspect of the movement toward fuller participation by women in American political affairs is the increasing proportion of offices they hold. While there are many explanations for this change, there are mainly two primary justifications why it should occur. The reason most often cited is simple fairness: the opportunities afforded women should equal the opportunities afforded men. This justification is essentially a normative statement not subject to empirical validation, though one might wish to assess the degree to which equal opportunity actually does exist. The second justification for increasing the number of women officeholders is that women bring a different perspective to public office and consequently behave differently than male officeholders would in certain situations. In a statement made prior to her retirement, former U. S. Representative Leonor Sullivan (D-Mo.) was asked to give her reaction to the increased number of women serving in Congress. She replied that she felt the change was beneficial for Congress because women are both more willing to compromise and more able to see where compromise is possible.[1]

The question of behavioral differences between male and female occupants of a different public office, trial judgeships, is the concern here. Specifically, can one detect behavioral differences between male and female judges in criminal cases, and can such differences explain the generally less severe sentences received by female defendants?

Potential behavioral differences between male and female judges are particularly great. Traditional sociological theory suggests that women approach the enforcement of cultural and group norms differently than men because of differences in sex role socialization.[2] Trial judges are explicitly concerned with norm enforcement.[3] Furthermore, much criminal behavior is in itself directly related to culturally defined sex role behavior,[4] and at least one offense, rape, is explicitly linked to sex and sex roles.[5] One question that will be examined, therefore, is whether accused rapists are treated differently by female judges than they are by male judges, the testable hypothesis being that women judges treat rapists more severely than do male judges.

In general, sociological theory leads to the expectation that women feel more threatened by challenges to norms and law than do men. Within the limits of their discretion, then, do female judges treat defendants (norm violators) more harshly than their male counterparts? Or, alternately, do female judges show more compassion and understanding than male judges, with the result that female judges treat defendants more leniently? The presence of general differences between male and female judges is another question to be explored. A failure to find differences may indicate that female and male judges are so constrained by factors such as plea bargaining that potential differences cannot come to the surface; or it may be an indication that variations related to the sex of the judge simply do not exist.

A further complication is the possible interaction between the sex of the judge and the sex of the defendant. Several studies have found that female defendants receive milder treatment than male defendants accused of similar offenses.[6] One explanation cited is differences in factors other than sex (prior record, specific nature of offense, etc.).[7] A recent analysis argued that the differences in treatment accorded male and female defendants could not be explained solely by these other factors, but rather that there was either a "chivalry" or "paternalism" factor at work; that is, male judges felt it necessary to treat female defendants differently than male defendants.[8] Whether such a difference represents "chivalry" or "paternalism" can be explored only after it has been found that these differences exist. If "chivalry" is a relevant factor, male judges would treat female defendants less harshly than male defendants, while female judges would treat male and female defendants the same. Such an effect will appear as a statistical interaction between the sex of the judge and the sex of the defendant. This is the last question to be addressed.

THE METRO CITY CRIMINAL COURT DATA

The data used to answer the questions raised above are drawn from the courts of one of the nation's principal urban areas, called for the sake of anonymity "Metro City."[9] Metro City has a number of unique features but also shares many common characteristics with other large urban centers. The metropolitan area is characterized by continued growth, while the core city itself is witnessing white flight, urban decay, and rising crime rates. Politically, the city is heavily Democratic, and economically it is characterized by fairly low measures of personal income and wealth. Along many dimensions, Metro City is representative of other large cities, and though a single sample point, there is no reason to believe that behavioral trends in this city would differ substantially elsewhere.

Metro City court is the principal trial court in the state's largest judicial district. Between July 1, 1968, and June 30, 1974, 62,436 cases were docketed and disposed of in the Metro City court. Of this total, 23,560 cases comprise the sample analyzed. Cases were deleted in two steps. The data file was constructed originally for a project with a somewhat different focus.[10] In building the file, cases were deleted if data central to the original study were missing.[11] Additional cases were then omitted if they fell into categories with too few cases for use in the present analysis. There is no evidence to suggest that the case deletion procedure has biased the sample in any way that would affect this investigation.

Operating within specific crime categories has been a standard approach to controlling for variations due to differing crime severities.[12] That is also the approach here, and cases were omitted because they fell into categories that included insufficient cases involving women defendants and/or women judges.[13] Only seven cases in the entire sample were lacking information on defendant's sex. No cases were lacking information on the trial judge's sex. The offense categories used are manslaughter (433 cases), robbery (5,250), aggravated assault (2,960), minor assault (2,678), larceny (3,890), forgery (1,064), drug offenses (6,187), and rape (886). Where more than one charge was involved, the charge that received the most severe sentence is analyzed. If several charges received the same sentence, the charge with the most severe potential sentence was selected.[14]

Since the focus of this analysis is specifically on judicial behavior, only decisions formally made by the trial judge are considered. Those decisions are judicial determinations of guilt and the imposition of sanctions. Two separate indicators of sentencing are used. There is a qualitative difference between sanctions of nonimprisonment (suspended sentence, probation, fine) and a jail term.[15] The critical decision to send a convicted offender to prison or hand down a less severe punishment is measured by a dichotomous variable jail/no jail. This choice was made in 17,276 cases. For 6,561 individuals (38%) the result was jail. The remaining 10,715 received lesser forms of punishment.

A second measure of sanctioning severity also deals with this subsample of 17,000-plus cases. This measure deemphasizes the breaking point between prison and nonimprisonment and instead taps subtler differences along a broader sanctioning continuum. In order to make meaningful distinctions between and among degrees of deprivation of individual freedom and the varying severity of nonprison sanctions, a detailed 93-point sentence severity scale was used. The scale breaks down into the following general categories (in increasing order of severity): (1) suspended sentences only (scale value 1); (2) fines only (scale values 2-6); (3) suspended sentences and fines (scale value 7-11); (4) probated sentences and probated sentences and fines (scale values 12-31); and (5) active jail sentences (scale values 32-93). This sentencing scale depicts a realistic spectrum of sanctioning alternatives. Since all but two of the 93 categories were employed, it is evident that judges both perceive and respond to the wide variety of sentencing possibilities available to them.

METHOD OF ANALYSIS

To facilitate contingency table analysis and also to test for the possible influence of extraneous factors, a new, four-category variable combining sex of the defendant and sex of the judge was created. This combined sex variable was then cross-tabulated with verdict, jail sentence, and average sentence severity; separate tables were constructed for each of the eight offense categories. Before proceeding to the analysis of the sex variables, it was necessary to determine if the analysis would be contaminated by omitted variables. Because of the infrequency of women defendants appearing before women judges, it was not possible to explicitly introduce further control variables into the statistical analysis. Previous work with the complete sample indicated that significant predictors of judicial behavior included offense severity, number of charges, and defendant's age.[16] To see if potential differences could be explained by variables other than sex of judge and defendant, 24 one-way analyses of variance were computed (three variables times eight offense categories). Ten of the 24 tests were significant with F values in the range of 4 to 15 (3 d.f. by 429 to 6184 d.f.). These relationships are described in Table 1. Their existence will necessitate particular care in interpreting the results presented below.

Using one of the techniques for complex contingency table analysis, the effects of the combined sex variable are partitioned into three components (sex of the defendant, sex of the judge, and the interaction of sex of judge and sex of defendant) to test the hypotheses outlined above.[17] Since the sentence severity variable is actually ordinal, the same statistical approach can also be used with the sentencing scale means.[18] Hence, the results for sentence severity make use of the chi square statistic rather than the more familiar F ratio.

ANALYSIS

There are three questions to be answered: Is the sex of the participants an important variable in criminal case dispositions? Is the behavior pattern of female judges any different than the behavior pattern of male judges? And, do judges respond differently to defendants of their own and the opposite sex? The first question is examined using the combined sex variable. The impact of this variable on each of the three dependent variables controlling for offense category is shown in Table 2. (The relevant subgroup percentages and subgroup means are shown in Table 4 which will be discussed below.) Regarding judicial determinations of guilt or innocence, the combined sex variable seems to have only a minor impact; it is significant only for robbery and drug offenses, and, as indicated by Cramer's V, in neither of these categories is the relationship strong. Statistically significant relationships between one of the components of the combined sex variable and judicial determinations of guilt may exist for manslaughter, aggravated assault, and larceny, but they are obscured by the inclusion of nonsignificant components of the combined variable. The exact nature of the various relationships will be examined below.

All of the fourteen possible relationships between sentencing behavior and the combined sex variable are statistically significant. While the relationships are significant in a statistical sense, the modest values for the Cramer's V and eta correlation coefficients indicate that the relationships are not particularly strong; the combined sex variable explains at most 5% of the variance in the sentencing scale. This suggests that while the sex of the participants does make some difference in the actual sentences received by criminal defend-

TABLE 1. Interpretation of Impact of Omitted Variables[a]

Charge	Relationship[b]	Expected Impact
Robbery	Female judges hear defendants with more charges	Female judges more likely to convict, jail, and sentence severely
Aggravated assault	Female defendants older	Female defendants should receive harsher sentences
	Female defendants are charged with fewer counts	Female defendants should receive less severe sentences
	Female judges handle defendants with more charges	Female judges more likely to convict, jail, and sentence severely
Minor assault	Female defendants older	Female defendants should receive harsher sentences
	Female defendants are charged with fewer counts	Female defendants should receive less severe sentences
Larceny	Female defendants older	Female defendants should receive harsher sentences
	Female defendants faced less severe charges	Female defendants should receive less severe sentences
Forgery	Female defendants younger	Female defendants should receive less severe sentences
Rape	Female judges handle defendants with more severe offenses	Female judges should be more likely to convict, jail, and sentence severely
Drugs	Female judges handle defendants with more counts	Female judges should be more likely to convict, jail, and sentence severely
	Female judges handle defendants with more serious charges	Female judges should be more likely to convict, jail, and sentence severely

[a]Omitted variables having a potential impact on those studied here include offense severity, number of charges, and defendant's age.
[b]The relationships reported in this table were found to be significant by means of a series of one-way analyses of variance; see the text for a discussion of the rationale behind these tests.

ants, other factors account for most of the variance in sentencing within offense categories.

A major point of interest is whether the sex of the trial judge has an effect on the disposition of criminal cases. As noted above, previous analyses have indicated that the defendant's sex can affect case disposition, both in terms of

TABLE 2. Overall Impact of Sex of Judge and Sex of Defendant

Offense	Verdict		Jail Sentence		Average Sentence Severity	
	χ^2	V^a	χ^2	V^a	F	eta[b]
Manslaughter	5.68[c]	.16	43.51[d]	.34	12.23	.17
Robbery	12.41	.06	34.79	.09	21.34	.13
Aggravated assault	7.41[c]	.06	68.19	.18	25.96	.19
Minor assault	2.41[c]	.04	41.00	.14	17.64	.16
Larceny	7.63[c]	.06	18.58	.08	8.19	.09
Forgery	0.54[c]	.04	22.80	.16	10.57	.18
Drugs	10.14	.05	35.35	.09	7.01	.07

[a]Cramers V; [b]Eta correlation coefficient; [c]Not significant at .05 level; [d]3 d.f.

TABLE 3. Disposition of Rape Cases by Sex of Judge

Sex of Judge	Percent Convicted by Judge	Percent of Those Convicted Sentenced to Jail	Average Sentence Severity[b]
Female	62.3%	48.1%	37.58
	(61)[a]	(54)	(54)
Male	52.5	44.5	36.28
	(503)	(519)	(519)
χ^2	2.10[c]	0.14[c]	—
t	—	—	0.41

[a]The number in parentheses is the N upon which the percentage or average is based.
[b]Average sentence severity based on 93-point sentence severity scale.
[c]Not significant at the .05 level.

verdicts and sentences. The effect of sex differences among judges has never been investigated empirically. Probably the most obvious situation where the sex of the judge might affect the outcome of a criminal proceeding is in a rape case. As Table 3 indicates, all three measures of judicial behavior used here indicate that female judges deal more harshly with rapists than male judges. However, none of the differences is statistically significant. Whatever actual differences may exist, they are too small to show up as significant with the number of cases included in the sample.

One interesting caveat that does not appear in Table 3 was the apparent tendency for rape cases in Metro City to be assigned to women judges more frequently than expected by chance. While women judges heard 4.5% of the cases in the entire sample of 43,000 + cases, they disposed of 9.7% of the rape cases; a single sample test of the deviation of a sample proportion (.097) from a population proportion (.045), yields a highly significant Z score of 7.47.

What about the other seven classes of cases included in the subsample; are there any differences between the behavior of female judges and the behavior of male judges? Of 21 possible relationships between disposition and sex of the judge (see Table 4), eight are statistically significant:

(1)   Female judges are more likely to convict in manslaughter cases.

(2) & (3) Female judges are more likely to convict in robbery cases *and* tend to impose severe sentences.

(4)   Female judges are *less* likely to convict in aggravated assault cases.

(5) & (6) Female judges are less likely to convict in larceny cases *but* tend to impose slightly more severe sentences on defendants who are convicted.

(7) & (8) Female judges impose harsher sentences in drug cases, *both* in terms of percent of defendants jailed and average sentence severity.

In all of these relationships, the sex of the defendant is controlled. Thus in six of 21 possible relationships, female judges are harsher than males; in two relationships female judges are less severe; and in thirteen there are no differences between male and female judges. Recall, however, that because of other factors found to influence sentencing, female judges are expected to be harsher in robbery, aggravated assault, and drug cases (see Table 1). Thus in four of the six relationships where female judges are more severe, this behavior is expected for reasons other than the sex of the judge. This leaves two relationships of greater female severity and two of greater leniency. Thus there is no strong evidence to suggest that female judges are consistently harsher with criminal defendants than are their male counterparts.

Consistent with previous studies, female defendants in this sample are treated differently than male defendants. Of 21 possible relationships, 18 are statistically significant; however, as previously noted, none are particularly strong. In terms of sentencing, every relationship between sex of the defendant and sentence received is statistically significant; four of the seven relationships between verdict determination by the judge are significant. In each instance, female defendants received less severe treatment than male defendants. Notably, most of these relationships remain even after taking into account the expected influence of other variables not explicitly introduced into the analysis (see Table 1).

The common sense explanation of differences in the treatment received by male and female defendants is the "chivalry" of male judges. If "chivalry" (or alternately paternalism) were the explanation, one should find that the sex differences in the treatment of defendants exist only for male judges and should be absent for female judges. Statistically, the "chivalry" factor would appear as a significant interaction between the sex of the judge and the sex of the defendant. As the "Interaction χ^2" tests in Table 4 indicate, there is no evidence of such a pattern; none of the 21 possible interactions is statistically significant. The more lenient treatment afforded female defendants cannot be explained as chivalry on the part of male judges.

TABLE 4. Sex of Judge and Defendant As Factors in Criminal Case Disposition

Charge	Sex of Defendant	Sex of Judge	Percent Convicted By Judge	N	Percent Jailed	Average Sentence Severity	N
Manslaughter	Female	Female	94.1%	8	14.3%	27.1	14
	Female	Male	68.2	44	22.9	25.7	60
	Male	Female	88.9	18	50.0	34.7	26
	Male	Male	75.9	166	62.5	38.9	264
	Defendant χ^2		n.s.[a]		56.26	54.31	
	Judge χ^2		7.27		n.s.	n.s.	
	Interaction χ^2[b]		n.s.		n.s.	n.s.	
Robbery	Female	Female	30.0%	10	57.1%	32.9	7
	Female	Male	50.0	88	41.8	26.3	91
	Male	Female	52.4	275	66.9	43.4	187
	Male	Male	59.9	2731	70.1	40.1	3496
	Defendant χ^2		5.04		28.83	168.81	
	Judge χ^2		6.83		n.s.	8.17	
	Interaction χ^2		n.s.		n.s.	n.s.	
Aggravated assault	Female	Female	38.5%	13	12.5%	15.9	8
	Female	Male	52.6	215	11.0	18.3	21
	Male	Female	48.5	130	45.4	28.6	49
	Male	Male	60.1	1749	40.4	26.4	716
	Defendant χ^2		4.84		140.97	163.88	
	Judge χ^2		7.57		n.s.	n.s.	
	Interaction χ^2		n.s.		n.s.	n.s.	
Minor assault	Female	Female	50.0%	4	20.0%	18.4	5
	Female	Male	63.6	228	7.3	12.8	205
	Male	Female	64.6	48	30.2	20.1	53
	Male	Male	67.9	1658	27.8	18.4	1788

			χ^2 / %	N	χ^2 / %	χ^2 / value	N
Larceny							
Defendant χ^2			n.s.		95.48	71.77	
Judge χ^2			n.s.		n.s.	n.s.	
Interaction χ^2			n.s.		n.s.	n.s.	
	Female	Female	33.3%	3	20.0%	18.4	5
	Female	Male	63.2	117	20.1	19.8	199
	Male	Female	44.4	45	43.1	26.8	65
	Male	Male	63.1	1855	33.4	22.1	2862
Forgery							
Defendant χ^2			n.s.		21.22	70.34	
Judge χ^2			7.20		n.s.	9.85	
Interaction χ^2			n.s.		n.s.	n.s.	
	Female	Female	66.7%	3	18.2%	23.0	11
	Female	Male	50.7	77	5.7	17.4	174
	Male	Female	60.0	10	22.2	24.4	27
	Male	Male	52.5	280	21.3	21.3	680
Drugs							
Defendant χ^2			n.s.		43.37	39.35	
Judge χ^2			n.s.		n.s.	n.s.	
Interaction χ^2			n.s.		n.s.	n.s.	
	Female	Female	41.1%	17	10.5%	18.6	19
	Female	Male	48.3	410	9.8	18.0	387
	Male	Female	48.3	147	30.3	22.9	119
	Male	Male	55.4	3513	20.8	19.4	3789
Defendant χ^2			7.23		48.74	12.92	
Judge χ^2			n.s.		3.86	9.78	
Interaction χ^2			n.s.		n.s.	n.s.	

[a] Not significant.
[b] The "Interaction χ^2" is a test of the "chivalry" hypothesis; see the text for a further discussion.

CONCLUSIONS

As is often the case, "common sense" hypotheses are not borne out when analyzed. Common sense, as well as sociological theory, suggests that the socialization experiences of men and women differ significantly. When those experiences are combined with cultural norms concerning the treatment of women by men, one should expect to find behavioral disparities on the bench. This analysis, however, indicates that the female judges in Metro City behave no differently than their male colleagues. This conclusion applies to their treatment of defendants in general and to their treatment of female defendants and rapists in particular.

One explanation of these "nonrelationships" lies in the women judges themselves. An examination of their career backgrounds indicates that all of the women judges in Metro City had "made it in a man's world." They all had served either as an assistant prosecuting attorney or as a deputy state attorney general (or both). All had been highly successful in the private practice of law. More than half had been part-time lecturers or instructors in law schools prior to judicial service. There is nothing to distinguish these careers from those of other successful attorneys, and the professional experiences of the women judges in Metro City perhaps diluted any effect that early sex role socialization experiences might have had. Furthermore, it may also be true that these women felt that they had to overcompensate and prove themselves in the predominantly male legal profession, further attenuating the effects of early experiences.

While this may explain the lack of overall differences, it does not account for the failure of the "chivalry" effect to appear. Even though women judges have probably made important accommodations in order to pursue a career in a male-dominated environment, it is unlikely that this has extended to being "chivalrous" vis-à-vis other women. One possible explanation for the absence of the chivalry effect may be the existence of another, unrelated phenomenon affecting women judges. While male judges are being "chivalrous," female judges may be influenced by something which might be called the "empathy" factor. Female judges may be more willing and better able to identify with and understand the problems that led women defendants to violate the law. This empathy, in turn, may have resulted in milder treatment of women defendants by women judges in a way that parallels the influence of chivalry on male judges. The existence of both a chivalry factor (for male judges) and an empathy factor (for female judges) would result in an overall trend of female defendants being treated less severely, which is exactly what this analysis finds. However, if there were two separate effects operating in tandem, it is unlikely that in every type of offense the two factors would have an identical effect; one would expect to find some differences in the effect of sex of the defendant depending upon the sex of the judge. No such differences appear.

There is a simpler explanation available. Psychological studies have shown that there seems "to be a deep-seated prohibition against inflicting physical pain on girls."[19] One study tested the willingness of college student subjects to administer electric shocks to other college students who were behaving in a deliberately uncooperative, irritating way. Both male and female subjects showed much greater reluctance to shock a confederate they thought was a woman.[20] This same prohibition may extend to other serious sanctions, such as those imposed by the criminal justice system. What is important is not the interaction of sex roles but simply the existence of sex roles; males are seen as better able to withstand sanctions and perhaps more deserving of punishment than females. This explanation is not the same as what has been called the chivalry factor because it does not depend upon one sex's perception of the other sex. It does, however, depend upon differences in the conceptions of the males and females. If this is the case, one should expect the differential treatment of female defendants to disappear as differences in the perceptions of sex roles decline.

Representative Sullivan may still be right. Women may bring both different perspectives and different behavior to most political offices. This generalization, however, fails to hold for the legal/political office that is a trial judgeship. While female judges in Metro City may well conceive of their role as differing markedly from that of their male colleagues, this difference, if it exists, does not translate into distinctive behavioral patterns. In Metro City the judicial sex attribute is not linked to an undesirable orthodoxy in a legal order designed to consider each case unique and on its own merits.

NOTES

Support for this analysis was provided by Rice University and the University of Missouri-St. Louis.

1. Statement given to the author, Aug. 31, 1976. Cong. Sullivan made a similar statement on the CBS radio network program, "Newsbreak P.M.," Mar. 9, 1976.

2. For example, see Talcott Parsons and Robert F. Bales, *Family, Socialization and Interaction Process* (New York: Free Press of Glencoe, 1955), pp. 3-131.

3. Herbert Jacob, *Justice in America* (Boston: Little, Brown, 1965), pp. 17-33.

4. See Richard A. Cloward and Lloyd E. Ohlin, *Delinquency and Opportunity* (New York: Free Press of Glencoe, 1960); and Gisela Konopka, *The Adolescent Girl in Conflict* (Englewood Cliffs, N. J.: Prentice-Hall, 1966).

5. See Susan Brownmiller, *Against Our Will: Men, Women and Rape* (New York: Simon and Schuster, 1975); and Andrea Medea and Kathleen Thompson, *Against Rape* (New York: Farrar, Straus, and Giroux, 1974).

6. See Stuart Nagel and Lenore Weitzman, "Women As Litigants," *Hastings Law Review*, vol. 23 (Nov. 1971), pp. 171-98; David N.

Atkinson and Dale A. Neuman, "Judicial Attitudes and Defendant Attributes: Some Consequences for Municipal Court Decision-Making," *Journal of Public Law*, vol. 19 (1970), pp. 78-79; and Carl E. Pope, *Sentencing of California Felony Offenders* (Washington, D. C.: Law Enforcement Assistance Administration, 1975), pp. 17-21.

7. John Hagan, "Extra-Legal Attributes and Criminal Sentencing: An Assessment of a Sociological Viewpoint," *Law & Society Review*, vol. 8 (Spring 1974), p. 375.

8. Elizabeth Moulds, "The Chivalry Factor and Disparities of Treatment in the Criminal Justice System," paper delivered to the 1976 Annual Meeting of the Southwestern Political Science Association, Dallas, Tex., Apr. 7-10, 1976.

9. Anonymity for the court under investigation was guaranteed as a precondition for access to these data.

10. See Thomas M. Uhlman, "Racial Justice: Black Judges and Defendants in the Metro City Criminal Court, 1968-1974" (Ph.D. dissertation, University of North Carolina, 1975).

11. See *ibid.*, pp. 145-51, for detailed infor-

mation on the case deletion criteria.

12. See Charles Engle, "Criminal Justice in the City: A Study of Sentence Severity and Variation in the Philadelphia Criminal Court System" (Ph.D. dissertation, Temple University, 1971); Edward Green, *Judicial Attitudes in Sentencing* (New York: St. Martin's Press, 1961), p. 26; and George W. Baab and William R. Furgeson, "Texas Sentencing Practices: A Statistical Study," *Texas Law Review,* vol. 45 (Feb. 1967), pp. 490-91.

13. This decision resulted in the omission of 20,142 cases included in the original project. See Uhlman, "Racial Justice," pp. 145-50.

14. See *ibid.,* pp. 151-55.

15. See Sheldon Glueck and Eleanor Glueck, *Ventures in Criminology* (Cambridge: Harvard University Press, 1964); and Peter Greenwood *et al., Prosecution of Adult Felony Defendants in Los Angeles County; A Policy Perspective* (Santa Monica, Calif.: Rand Corporation, 1973), p. xi.

16. See Uhlman, "Racial Justice," pp. 441-90.

17. The technique used here is that described by James Grizzle, C. Frank Starmer, and Gary C. Koch, "Analysis of Categorical Data by Linear Models," *Biometrics,* vol. 25 (1969), pp. 489-504; the computer program used is NONMET II, described by Herbert M. Kritzer, "NONMET II: A Program for the Analysis of Contingency Tables and Other Types of Nonmetric Data by Weighted Least Squares," *Behavior Research Methods and Instrumentation,* vol. 8 (June 1976), pp. 20-21.

18. See Robert G. Lehnen and Gary G. Koch, "A General Linear Approach to the Analysis of Non-metric Data: Applications for Political Science," *American Journal of Political Science,* vol. 18 (May 1974), pp. 283-313.

19. Eleanor Maccoby and Carol Jacklin, *The Psychology of Sex Differences* (Stanford, Calif.: Stanford University Press, 1974), p. 332.

20. S. P. Taylor and S. Epstein, "Aggression As a Function of the Interaction of the Sex of the Aggressor and the Sex of the Victim," *Journal of Personality,* vol. 35 (1967), pp. 474-96.

LAURA KATZ OLSON
Lehigh University

Sex-Linked Values: Their Impacts on Women in Engineering

The number of employed women in the United States has steadily increased over the years, and by 1970 nearly 43% of the female population 16 years and over was working outside the home.[1] However, while the 1960 census shows that women accounted for 65% of the increase in the labor force between 1950 and 1960, in professional fields women comprised only 26% of this increase.[2] By 1970, women accounted for only 39% of professional and technical workers, of which 70% were in nursing or noncollege teaching. Women are conspicuously absent in the high paying and/or high prestige occupations usually considered professional. By 1969, women accounted for only 8% of natural scientists, 10% of mathematicians, 3% of lawyers, 6% of the clergy, 7% of doctors, and 2% of dentists.[3]

Engineering, however, is the most male dominated profession in the United States and is also proving unusually resistant to change. According to one source, 8% of the female population, compared to 12% of males, appear to have engineering aptitudes.[4] Yet only 1.2% of engineers were women in 1950, and the percentage decreased to .8% in 1960 and to .5% by 1970. Presently, approximately .8% of the profession consists of females. These percentages are apt to be even lower, since a significant number of the females lack university degrees and even high school diplomas. These individuals are presumably practicing as technicians rather than as professional engineers.[5]

Recently, deans of engineering schools, academicians, university admission officers, and others have attempted to assess why there are so few women engineers in this country. However, rather than address themselves to the economic, institutional, and structural barriers, these individuals have tended to focus on the social, political, and psychological predispositions of women themselves. The prevailing assumption appears to be that the paucity of women in engineering is the result of a "lack of congruence" between women's values and those prevailing in the engineering profession. Emphasis on female psychology and values not only diverts attention from solving crucial problems, but also results in misplaced efforts at recruitment.

Scholars who have studied occupational attitudes and values tend to agree that engineers consist of a narrow range of personality types. They are viewed generally as thing-oriented, rather than people-oriented, nonverbal, conservative, and uninterested in social problems.[6] Stanley Robin reports, "The sociological and psychological research available concerning engineering specifically lead us to the conclusion that engineers, while professionally dedicated, are narrow of interest, stolid, relatively uninterested in 'cultural' things and are not inclined to general intellectual pursuits."[7] In a study of engineers and administrators working for a large nonmilitary aerospace contractor, Arnold Auerbach supports the conclusion that "engineers—at least those at the managerial level—are generally less concerned with social issues than with economic ones."[8] While engineers tend to have a strong commitment to technical achievements, the social implications are clearly secondary. Moreover, a study of mass culture by Harold Wilensky points out that engineers score significantly lower than other professionals on exposure to quality magazines, books, newspapers, and television programs. In reading about political news, engineers scored about the same as lower white-collar workers.[9]

While research indicates that strong and stable relationships tend to exist between values and occupations,[10] there is also an assumption, often unsubstantiated by concrete analysis, that values are sex-linked and remain so regardless of occupational choice. It is asserted that these value differences inhibit or encourage the entrance of women into certain occupations (or subfields within an occupation) and that males and females pursue different sources of satisfaction from their work experiences. For example, one observer notes, "But why are women scientists so few, and why do so many talented women stay away from science? . . . It may be the *naturally humanistic* instinct of women which leaves them ill at ease with the organization of science as we know it today."[11] Stanley Robin, in his article "The Female in Engineering" asserts:

Intellectual sophistication, defined as broad interests, emotional sensitiveness, a 'liberal arts' approach to learning, responsiveness to art and literature, and relative tolerance of intellectual creativity and deviation, seems to be a salient characteristic of academically oriented females . . . . The outlook of engineers, the sort of persons self-selected, and presumably the socialization compatible with and reinforcing of the characteristics of engineers are fundamentally incompatible with the interests, aspirations, and personal characteristics of females who would otherwise select the field for an occupational career.[12]

It is thus suggested that feminine characteristics, such as people-orientation, interest in social, artistic, and creative pursuits, and the low priority of monetary rewards, are incongruent with the dominant occupational expectations of engineering.[13]

Difficulties which women students face in engineering schools, and later in their professional experiences, are also attributed to value differences and other personal characteristics of females. For example, the director of advising and counseling at Cornell's College of Engineering stated that women experience difficulty in engineering because they embrace values that are foreign to an educational institution and a profession that has a "masculine" norm.[14] Similarly, a female engineering professor observed, "The stress of a difficult curriculum combined with female emotions and psychology create a set of problems that are new to most engineering faculty."[15] An associate dean of an engineering college asserted, "I was convinced that problems developed because females entering engineering differed greatly in their attitudes and expectations from their male counterparts."[16] Therefore, the high attrition rates of female engineering students, as compared to males, are assumed to be related to the stifling or restrictive nature of the technical curriculum, which is antagonistic to the females' nurturing, humanistic, and people-oriented impulses.

Finally, arguments expressing the need for more women engineers, as well as efforts to recruit females, are often based on the assumption that females have a different contribution to make to the profession than men. Margaret Mead suggests that engineering loses "the balancing and complementary values gained by the differing approaches of the two sexes to the same problem."[17] Irene Peden, an associate dean of engineering, agrees: "Women tend to be more people-oriented than men . . . . They have a special sensitivity to the needs of others, and often outperform men where patience and efforts toward harmony are concerned . . . . [They] can bring new dimensions to the 'masculine' professions." [18] In a similar vein, Charles F. Horne, chairman of the board of the Southern California Industry-Education Council, suggests, "Women engineers have more understandingly utilized their knowledge for what I would call 'engineering for the humanities,' as distinct from engineering only for engineering's sake."[19] Another student of the subject notes that "one of the most important forms of action open to women in engineering will undoubtedly be in the area of social improvements."[20] Much of the literature on women and engineering goes on in a similar vein.[21]

These assumptions are not only used as a justification for the segregation of women in a limited number of engineering subfields and job categories, but they also have the effect of reinforcing these concentrations. For example, women engineers are found primarily in research, development, and design rather than in production, construction, administration, and management, the former categories tending to be those with lesser pay, promotional opportunities, prestige, and decision-making power. Moreover, without addressing themselves to the real issues and concerns of women, those individuals involved with recruitment will encounter limited success.

This article seeks to explore whether in fact women have different interests, values, and occupational expectations from men which presumably contribute both to the paucity of females entering an engineering curriculum, and to the higher attrition rates of female engineering students as compared to male engineering students.

THE STUDY

It is hypothesized that (1) differences in values, interests, and work expectations between males and females are minimal and therefore do not contribute substantially to the paucity of female engineering students; and (2) similar orientations will be found in male and female engineering students. Therefore, sex-linked differences in values, interests, and work expectations are not a major factor in the higher attrition rates of women engineering students.

In June 1975, an interdisciplinary workshop on "Women and Engineering" was instituted at Lehigh University, consisting of six faculty and twelve undergraduates. As part of the workshop, four faculty members conducted a 132-question survey which was administered through face-to-face interviews to 191 Lehigh undergraduates. The sample was divided into four subsamples, with respondents randomly selected within each category. These included male engineering students, female engineering students, male nonengineering students, and female nonengineering students. These were further stratified by class. The overall response rate was over 90%. The purpose of the questionnaire was to assess multidimensional issues and problems surrounding women in engineering. The aim of this article is to compare attitudes, interests, and professional expectations between male and female Lehigh University students as well as those among the three colleges—Engineering, Liberal Arts, and Business.

FINDINGS

Several studies of the engineering profession have portrayed it as having a "conservative bias."[22] In order to assess whether female students, in general, and female engineering students, in particular, have political orientations antagonistic to those of the engineering profession, as well as to compare views among the survey groups, respondents were asked to indicate whether they consider themselves liberal, moderate, or conservative. Since the concern here was with self-perceived values, objective measurements would not have been useful.

Turning to Table 1, the data do not show a significant relationship between political identification and sex. However, a slightly higher percentage of males than females in the sample can be seen at both extremes of the political spectrum. Thirty percent of the males are liberal and 24% are conservative, as compared with 22% and 17%, respectively, of the females. Moreover, 60% of the women define themselves as moderates. The data present little evidence that the female's political views are more at variance with the engineering norm than males and weaken the claim that females do not choose the profession because they see it as too conservative.

When political views are compared by college, the evidence indicates that business students tend to be the most conservative, followed by engineering students. Liberal arts majors perceive themselves as the most liberal group. These percentages tend to remain essentially the same for liberal arts majors, controlling for sex, but there is some variation between males and females within the engineering college. A larger percentage of males are liberal, while a larger percentage of females are moderates.[23] Since female engineering students appear more in conformity than males with the engineering political norm, political views appear not to be a crucial factor in the higher attrition rates of women.

Although the relationship between college and political orientation is not significant, the larger differences among professionals might be the result of occupational socialization, which consists of learning the prevailing informal values and attitudes. A research review of women in science and engineering,

TABLE 1. Self-Evaluation of Political View

	Liberal	Moderate	Conservative	D.K.	Totals
A. Sex					
Males (N = 98)	30%	43%	24%	3%	100% $X^2 = 6.27$
Females (N = 92)	22	60	17	1	100 n.s.
B. College					
Engineering (N = 98)	24	55	18	3	100 $X^2 = 10.51$
Liberal Arts (N = 58)	33	50	14	3	100 n.s.
Business (N = 34)	18	44	38	0	100
C. Engineering College					
Males (N = 50)	32	44	20	4	100 $X^2 = 4.71$
Females (N = 48)	17	65	17	1	100 n.s.
D. Liberal Arts College					
Males (N = 23)	35	44	13	8	100 $X^2 = 3.43$
Females (N = 35)	31	54	14	1	100 n.s.
E. Business College					
Males (N = 25)	20	40	40	0	100 $X^2 = .74$
Females (N = 9)	11	56	33	0	100 n.s.
TOTAL N = 190					

for example, found that "values can be shaped to fit the career; that the career-relevant attributes need not exist in advance."[24] Moreover, since males and females are concentrated in different occupations and work roles within occupations, differences between male and female professionals may become enlarged.

It is interesting to note that half of the respondents view engineering students as conservative, including engineering students themselves (see Table 2). Moreover, male nonengineers perceive engineering students as *more* conservative than female nonengineers. Further, the percentage of female liberal arts students indicating that engineers are conservative is lower than any of the other survey groups. In fact, nearly a third of the female liberal arts majors profess that they do not even know the political views of engineering students.

Moreover, while male and female engineering students have a similar picture of engineering students' political views, these are vastly different from their self-perceived identifications, regardless of sex. Thirty-two percent of the males indicate that they are liberal and 20% conservative, yet none view engineers as liberal, and 46% perceive them as conservative. Similarly, 17% of the female engineers view themselves as conservative and 17% as liberal, while only 4% view engineers as liberal and 50% as conservative.

The data do not suggest, therefore, that female engineering students are more susceptible than male engineering students to a conflict between their own political views and those they perceive existing among their colleagues. Nor does it show that females, in general, perceive greater dissonance than males between their own political values and those of engineering majors.

It has been suggested that women have broader interests than men, such as social, cultural, and artistic pursuits, which are antagonistic to the rigid and narrow requirements of the technical curricula. One student of the subject notes that women express more diversity of interests than men entering technical curricula. The men are more narrow and geared to technical concerns alone. While substantially more women than men drop out of technical schools for this reason, those females who persist "[reduce] their technical credit load and [find] an extra-curricular activity to satisfy their interests outside of technology."[25]

In order to look at these premises, a comparison was made of extracurricular activities among the survey groups. Respondents were asked to indicate whether they are involved in any organizations or groups at Lehigh or in the Lehigh Valley community, as well as to name the two most important ones. The data showed that an overwhelming majority of all students participate in extracurricular activities with no measurable differences among the survey groups. Table 3 tabulates the results of those reporting participation in two organizations by type of activities. Although females, in general, are more interested in volunteer work and men in sports, there are no other measurable differences between the sexes. Twenty percent of the males and 18% of the females indicated social organizations, 8% and 10% political, 44% and 47% arts/communications, and 26% and 24% academics. The data, therefore, do

TABLE 2. Perception of Engineering Students' Political Views

	Liberal	Moderate	Conservative	D.K.	Totals
A. Sex					
Males (N = 98)	5%	30%	53%	12%	100% $X^2 = 1.57$ n.s.
Females (N = 92)	3	34	47	16	100 n.s.
B. College					
Engineering (N = 98)	6	38	48	8	100 $X^2 = 16.39$ p.01
Liberal Arts (N = 58)	2	24	47	27	100 p.01
Business (N = 34)	3	27	62	8	100
C. Engineering College					
Males (N = 50)	8	40	46	6	100 $X^2 = 1.39$ n.s.
Females (N = 48)	4	35	50	11	100 n.s.
D. Liberal Arts College					
Males (N = 23)	0	17	57	26	100 $X^2 = 2.22$ n.s.
Females (N = 35)	3	29	40	28	100 n.s.
E. Business College					
Males (N = 25)	4	20	64	12	100 $X^2 = 3.01$ n.s.
Females (N = 9)	0	44	56	0	100 n.s.
TOTAL N = 190					

TABLE 3. Involvement in Extracurricular Activities, By Type of Activity

	Volunteer	Social	Political	Arts/Comm.	Sports	Academic	Other	Totals
A. Sex								
Males (N = 67)	10%	20%	8%	44%	68%	26%	24%	200%[a]
Females (N = 67)	36	18	10	46	48	24	18	200
B. Engineering College								
Males (N = 35)	18	16	8	38	60	40	20	200
Females (N = 32)	34	10	4	44	54	40	14	200
TOTAL N = 134								

[a]Totals = 200% since they include the two most important extracurricular activities for each respondent.

not support the assumption that women have more cultural, social, and/or artistic interests than men which would lead them to view the engineering curricula as too narrow.

Among engineers, there are no significant sex-linked extracurricular interests. Males and females are relatively uninvolved in the social and political categories and equally interested in arts/communications, academic organizations and sports. It should also be noted that 40% of the female engineering students indicated participation in an academic organization related to engineering and other "technical" interests. Thus female engineering students do not seem to have broader leisure time concerns than male engineering students in order to compensate for the rigidities of the technical program.

To further explore these issues, the engineering students were asked: "Which gives you more satisfaction, your school work or things you do in your spare time?" Table 4 shows that female engineering students, as compared to male engineering students, get *more* staisfaction in their school work than in their extracurricular activities. While 43% of the females chose school work, only 28% of the males selected this item. These findings substantiate the previous observation that female engineering students do not appear to be utilizing extracurricular activities more than male engineering students as a means of coping with the technical curricula.

Respondents were also asked how satisfied they are with their major. Table 5 shows that nearly all of the respondents, including female engineering students, are satisfied with their present curricula. Only 6% of the female engineers express some dissatisfaction. In fact, the most dissatisfied group appears to be female liberal arts students, despite their more flexible programs. Female engineering students, therefore, do not perceive themselves as more dissatisfied with their courses than do either male engineers or other females. The engineering curriculum does not appear to contribute to the higher attrition rates of female engineering students.

It also has been assumed that academic males and females differ in their approaches to learning and professional goals. The arguments that women have broader interests than males and are more inclined to the liberal arts have been used to justify the limited number of females selecting engineering, as well as the large percentage switching from the field to other programs.

In order to further test these assertions, the students were asked about their expectations of a college education. Table 6 reports the evidence. There are no significant sex-linked differences. The majority of both males and females perceive career preparation rather than "exposure to new ideas," as the primary goal of higher education. Only 29% of the females and 17% of the males selected the latter category.

Moreover, within each of the three colleges there were no measurable differences between the sexes. Although it can be argued that women chose "exposure to new ideas" more often than men, regardless of college, these differentials range from only 5% for the business college, 13% for the engineering college, and 14% for the arts college. The data therefore suggest that women

TABLE 4. "Which Gives You More Satisfaction, Your School Work or Things You Do In Your Spare Time?"

	Male Engineering Students (N = 50)	Female Engineering Students (N = 47)
School work	28%	43%
Spare time	70	49
D.K.	2	8
TOTALS	100%	100%

N = 97
$X^2 = 5.25$: n.s.

TABLE 5. Satisfaction With One's Major

	Engineering		Liberal Arts		Business	
	Male (N = 49)	Female (N = 48)	Male (N = 20)	Female (N = 28)	Male (N = 19)	Female (N = 7)
Satisfied	88%	81%	85%	75%	85%	100%
Neither satisfied nor dissatisfied	8	13	5	7	15	0
Dissatisfied	4	6	10	18	0	0
TOTALS	100%	100%	100%	100%	100%	100%
	$X^2 = 2.63$: n.s.		$X^2 = .88$: n.s.		$X^2 = 1.31$: n.s.	

TOTAL N = 171

TABLE 6. Expectations of a College Education

	Exposure to New Ideas	Career Prep.	Attainment of Degree	Opportunity for Social Life	Satisfy Parents	Totals	
A. Sex							
Males (N = 98)	17%	63%	18%	1%	1%	100%	X^2 = 8.07
Females (N = 92)	29	62	8	0	1	100	n.s.
B. College							
Engineering (N = 98)	14	73	12	1	0	100	X^2 = 17.29
Liberal Arts (N = 58)	35	47	16	0	2	100	p. .05
Business (N = 34)	29	59	12	0	0	100	
C. Engineering College							
Males (N = 50)	8	74	16	2	0	100	X^2 = 4.99
Females (N = 48)	21	71	8	0	0	100	n.s.
D. Liberal Arts College							
Males (N = 23)	26	44	26	0	4	100	X^2 = 3.69
Females (N = 35)	40	49	9	0	2	100	n.s.
E. Business College							
Males (N = 25)	28	56	16	0	0	100	X^2 = 1.63
Females (N = 9)	33	67	0	0	0	100	n.s.

TOTAL N = 190

TABLE 7. Reasons for Career Choice

	Extrinsic	Intrinsic	Intellectual	People-Oriented	Other	Totals
A. Sex						
Males (N = 81)	27%	55%	3%	8%	7%	100%
Females (N = 82)	20	56	5	13	6	100
B. Engineering College						
Males (N = 45)	27	56	3	6	8	100
Females (N = 45)	21	56	8	6	9	100

TOTAL N = 163

are no more likely than men to perceive college as a broadening experience and thus no more likely to avoid the technical curricula for this reason.

However, the data show a significant relationship between the respondents' college and their expectations. Male and female engineering students have expectations different from those of liberal arts and business majors. Over 70% of the engineering students chose career preparation, as compared to 47% of liberal arts and 59% of business students. Only 21% of the female and 8% of the male engineering respondents indicated "exposure to new ideas." This suggests that the liberal arts approach to education is essentially antagonistic to the interests of engineering students, regardless of sex.

To look at professional goals, the students were asked to indicate the two most important reasons for choosing their careers. Several studies have divided these goals into four categories, which include intrinsic, intellectual, extrinsic, and people-orientation. Intrinsic includes self-satisfaction and general interest in the subject. Opportunity to be creative and original are intellectual reasons, while chances for advancement, job opportunities, and financial rewards are some examples of extrinsic ones. Opportunities to be helpful to others and to society are people-oriented explanations. It has been suggested that females tend to choose careers primarily for people-oriented reasons and males for extrinsic rewards. Since engineering is perceived as "thing-oriented" rather than "people-oriented," the profession is presumably not desirable to females.[26]

Turning to Table 7, the data again do not show significant sex-linked differences. A majority of all students, regardless of sex, chose intrinsic, while only 13% of the females and 8% of the males selected people-oriented goals. Thus the assumption that women are primarily interested in helping others while men are concerned with salary and advancement (extrinsic goals) is not confirmed by the data.

Male and female engineering students have similar reasons for choosing their careers. Intrinsic rewards were stated 56% of the time by both sexes. It is important to note that the major intrinsic reasons given by the engineering students were "thing-oriented" ones. Intellectual explanations and "to help others" were given less than 10% of the time by the engineers, regardless of sex. Thus the goals of female engineering students not only are similar to male engineering students, but they also appear in conformity with those of the profession.

CONCLUSIONS AND RECOMMENDATIONS FOR CHANGE

It is not the intent of this article to suggest that there are inconsequential differences in values and interests between male and female engineering students, or between males and females in general. Clearly it would be impossible for individuals to overcome entirely the sexist socialization process which stresses different orientations for males and females. However, this research suggests that much of the literature on women and engineering has overstated and simplified these complex differences and has overemphasized their impacts on the paucity of females in engineering schools as well as on the high attrition rates of female engineering students. Thus, efforts at recruitment have been misdirected, and major obstacles keeping women out of the profession have not been scrutinized adequately.

Where does one go from here? Future research should focus on means for overcoming substantial barriers that prevent women from entering engineering as well as those inducing female engineering students to leave engineering programs. Although it is not an exhaustive list, the following items are suggestive of areas in need of special attention:

(1) There is some indication that female engineering students have a greater difficulty in the financing of their education than male engineering students, women nonengineering students, and male nonengineering students.[27] If this is substantiated by further study, grants earmarked for women in technical programs will be required.

(2) Engineering is not even an option unless students have good foundations in mathematics and science before they enter college. Women must be encouraged in elementary school to take these courses. There is some evidence that girls are discouraged and even prevented from taking advanced mathematics- and science-oriented courses.[28] Moreover, it is suspected that guidance counselors tend to direct talented women away from technical careers. Thus, university-sponsored educational programs aimed at teachers, guidance counselors, and grade school children could prove rewarding.

(3) Traditional fields open to women, such as teaching, have become less accessible, while engineering jobs are readily available. Moreover, engineering has one of the highest starting salaries of all professions not requiring an advanced degree. Are these facts known to women, and what programs can be set up to publicize them?

(4) What roles have the federal government and the economy played in discouraging females from entering the profession? Answers and solutions must be found.

(5) There is some evidence that female engineering students are faced with social isolation. Often they are left out of student study sessions or have less access to other students' notes than males. Since engineering schools tend to have so few females, often due to sexist selective admission processes, this situation is inevitable. Means for overcoming the social isolation issue must be investigated. Some solutions might be for engineering schools to admit a "critical mass" of females each year, to house them together, and/or to provide special classes for discussing problems of women in engineering. Moreover, quotas for women must be eliminated.

(6) Once in college, it is difficult for students generally to transfer into engineering programs. Means should be found for easing this process.

(7) It would appear crucial that female engineering students have female role models. Greater efforts are needed to recruit women to engineering faculties and to invite women speakers to college campuses.

(8) An effort should be made to assess attitudes of male engineering faculty toward their female students and to find means for overcoming negative ones. Moreover, female guidance counselors might be utilized to provide positive reinforcements.

(9) Despite affirmative action efforts, many engineering firms still refuse to hire women. Many females who do find employment, even jobs with high starting salaries, encounter severe difficulties with promotional opportunities and salary increases. These issues require study.

Females account for an extremely low percentage of high paying and/or high prestige professional and technical workers in the United States. However, engineering, consisting of less than 1% females, is the most male-dominated. Thus it is a crucial occupation to study if one is to understand the dynamics of sexism in the professions, and it is necessary that future research on women and work should go beyond sex-linked differences in values and work expectations. To account for the paucity of women in certain fields, one must focus instead on the institutional barriers which are an integral part of our political, economic, and social system. Society cannot afford to underutilize one-half of its population, and women cannot afford to be underutilized. Substantial time and effort will be necessary to break down these bastions of male dominance.

NOTES

1. Francine D. Blau, "Women in the Labor Force: An Overview," in *Women: A Feminist Perspective*, ed. Jo Freeman (Palo Alto, Calif.: Mayfield, 1975), p. 217.

2. A. S. Rossi, "Barriers to the Career Choice of Engineering, Medicine or Science Among American Women," in *Women and the Scientific Professions*, eds. J. A. Mattfeld and G. G. Van Aken (Cambridge, Mass.: MIT Press, 1965), p. 65.

3. Barbara Deckard, *The Women's Movement* (New York: Harper and Row, 1975), pp. 113-14.

4. Kirsten Amundsen, *The Silenced Majority* (Englewood Cliffs, N. J.: Prentice-Hall, 1971), p. 34.

5. U. S., Women's Bureau Bulletin, *Employment Opportunities for Women in Professional Engineering* (Washington, D. C.: Government Printing Office, 1954).

6. "Engineers: An Examination of Some Myths and Contradictions Concerning Engineers," *Science For the People*, vol. 3 (May 1973), pp. 16-20; and J. Melissa Brown, "A Woman in the World of Engineering," *IEEE Transactions on Education*, vol. E-18 (Feb. 1975), pp. 3-10.

7. Stanley S. Robin, "The Female in Engineering," in *The Engineers and the Social System*, eds. Robert Perrucci and Joel E. Gerstl (New York: Alfred A. Knopf, 1969), p. 35.

8. Arnold J. Auerbach, "Are Minorities and Women Really As Inefficient as White Engineers Say?" *New Engineer*, vol. 22 (Jan. 1975), p. 30.

9. Harold L. Wilensky, "Mass Society and Mass Culture: Interdependence or Independence?" *American Sociological Review*, vol. 29 (Apr. 1964), pp. 173-97.

10. See, for example, James Davis, *Great Aspirations* (Chicago: Aldine, 1964); and Carolyn Perrucci, "Sex-Based Professional Socialization Among Graduate Students in Science," in *Research Issues in the Employment of Women: Proceedings of a Workshop* (Washington, D. C.: n.p., Sept. 23-24, 1974).

11. Dolly Ghosh, "Introduction to Women in Science," *Impact*, vol. 25 (Apr.-June 1975), pp. 99-103. Emphasis added.

12. Robin, pp. 210-11.

13. See, for example, Deborah S. David, *Career Patterns and Values: A Study of Men and Women in Science and Engineering* (Washington, D. C.: n.p., Nov. 1971); Ravenna Helson, "Personality Characteristics and Sex in Science," in *Research Issues in the*

Employment of Women, pp. 63-82; Mary Diederich Ott, "Attitudes and Experiences of Freshmen Engineers at Cornell," in *Women in Engineering: Beyond Recruitment,* eds. Mary Ott and Nancy Reese (Ithaca, N. Y.: Cornell University Press, 1975), pp. 13-19; and Joyce I. Medalen, "Women in Engineering — 1 Percent to 10 Percent in Four Years," *IEEE Transactions on Education,* pp. 38-40.

14. Robert E. Gardner, "Women: The New Engineers," in Ott and Reese, pp. 158-70.

15. Medalen, "Women in Engineering," p. 40.

16. Malcolm Burton, "Introduction" to *Women in Engineering: Beyond Recruitment,* by Ott and Reese, p. 3.

17. Margaret Mead, quoted in Robert Amon, "Engineering in Short Supply," *Industrial Bulletin,* vol. 30 (June 1963), p. 2.

18. Irene C. Peden, "New Faces of Eve: Women in Electrical Engineering," *IEEE Spectrum,* vol. 26 (Apr. 1968), p. 82.

19. Charles F. Horne, quoted in Naomi J. McAfee, "Brighter Prospects for Women in Engineering," *The American Society for Engineering Education,* vol. 32 (Apr. 1974), p. 9.

20. Josette de Bellefonds, "Women and Engineering," *Impact of Science on Society,* vol. 14 (Nov. 1964), p. 254.

21. See also Ronna Y. Toba, "Recipe For a Science Happening," *IEEE Transactions on Education,* pp. 20-24; and Thelma Estrin, "Ms. Biomedical Engineer: A New Professional Opportunity for Women," *IEEE Transactions on Education,* pp. 11-14.

22. See, for example, J. Melissa Brown, "Women in the World of Engineering," p. 5.

23. Throughout this report, comparisons between males and females in the business college will not be made since the female N for the business college is too small for fruitful analysis (N = 9).

24. Cora Marrett, "Women in Science and Engineering: A Research Review," *Research Issues in the Employment of Women,* pp. 10-11.

25. Sandra O. Davis, "A Researcher's Eye View: Women Students, Technical Majors and Retention," *IEEE Transactions on Education,* pp. 25-29.

26. See, for example, James Davis, *Great Aspirations,* and David, "Career Patterns."

27. See, for example, Engin Inel Holmstrom, "The New Pioneers: Women Engineering Students," paper presented to the Workshop for the Female Engineering Undergraduate — Beyond Recruitment, Ithaca, N. Y., June 24-27, 1975.

28. Margaret E. Law, "The Problems Facing Women Scientists and Engineers in Academia — A Review," in Ott and Reese, pp. 40-49.

SUSAN A. MACMANUS
University of Houston

NIKKI R. VAN HIGHTOWER
Women's Advocate for the City of Houston

The Impacts of Local Government Tax Structures on Women: Inefficiencies and Inequalities

Due at least partially to the passage of the Equal Pay Act of 1963, Title VII of the 1964 Civil Rights Act, and the entire Women's Movement, a considerable literature has been produced over the past decade discussing the economically disadvantaged position of women.[1] Much research has also been done regarding the fiscal structures of local governments, which have increasingly become strained.[2] These studies have focused attention on the inadequacies of local government tax structures, particularly the regressiveness of local property taxes. To date, however, there have been virtually no attempts to determine whether the economically disadvantaged position of women, especially in the large metropolitan areas of the U. S., affects local government tax structures or, conversely, whether local government tax structures affect the economic positions of women.

The purposes of this paper include, first, a comparison of the per capita personal incomes of women and men in order to determine the extent of income inequality. Secondly, a comparison will be made of the tax burdens borne by each of these groups in an attempt to establish whether there is a linkage between income inequalities and local government tax structures. Finally, an examination of the relationship between tax burdens and levels of service provision will be made to determine the efficiency (or inefficiency) of local government tax structures on men and women. The results of this analysis should provide some insights into the question of the equity and efficiency of local government tax structures as regards economic imbalances between males and females in American society.

RESEARCH DESIGN

The linkages between per capita personal income, local government tax burdens (total, property, and nonproperty), tax efficiencies, and different male and female household-status groups were examined through comparison of means analysis, using two controls: region and population size. The units of analysis were the Standard Metropolitan Statistical Areas with populations of 250,000 or more (n = 125). The period for which the analysis was performed was the year 1972.

Data. Population and socioeconomic data were collected from the *U. S. Census of Population, 1970.* Financial (revenue and expenditure) data were collected from the *U. S. Census of Governments, 1972.*

Types of Household-Status Groups. One of the early results of the study was the discovery that the U. S. Bureau of the Census categorization of income earners is somewhat sexist. The major categories of household-status are: Male Heads of Household (married males living with wives and other family members); Primary Males (single males); Female Heads of Household (women living without spouse but with other family members); Wives of heads (women living with spouse and other family members); Primary females (single females). It should be noted that with the exception of the primary group designation, the male and female household-status groups are not comparable. This results from the U. S. Census Bureau's usage of the term "head of household," of which there can be only one per family and, if there is a male present, the male must be so designated. As stated by the Census Bureau, "One person in each household is designated as the 'head,' that is, the person who is regarded as the head by the members of the household. However, if a married woman living with her husband was reported as the head, her husband was considered the head for the purpose of simplifying the tabulation."[3]

Thus, male "heads of household" includes all males living with family members whether or not a spouse is present. Since by Census Bureau definition there can be only one head, the comparable group of females must be divided into two categories: (1) "Wife of Head" for those women living with spouses; and (2) Female "Heads of Household" for those women living without spouses but with other members of their families.

Control Groups. Control groups utilized in this study included region and population size. Since cost of living adjustments were not available by SMSA, the closest approximation to such an adjustment can be made by analyzing the data by region. The regional classification scheme adopted for this study was the standard Bureau of the Census classification: Northeast; South; North Central (Midwest); and West.

Similarly, controls for differences in economies of scale were virtually unobtainable for SMSA units of analysis. Consequently, the "best" surrogate measure for economies of scale was population size. The SMSA's have been grouped into three population size categories: 1,000,000 and over; 500,000-999,999; and 250,000-499,999. The exclusion of SMSA's under 250,000 population is solely a function of data availability. The Census Bureau does not report income by sex and household-status for SMSA's under 250,000 population.

Tax Structure Measures. The two tax structure measures focused upon by this study were tax burdens (total, property, and nonproperty) and tax efficiency (of all services and of poverty-linked services, such as welfare, health, hospitals, and housing and urban renewal). Tax burden (or effort) was defined in terms of the relationship between per capita tax revenue and per capita personal income. In other words, the total tax burden was calculated by dividing per capita property tax revenue and per capita nonproperty tax revenue, respectively, by per capita personal income.

Tax efficiency (the service-tax burden ratio) was defined in terms of the relationship between the benefits an individual or household receives from the expenditures of the government and the tax burden he or she bears as a result of the government's taxation policies. To derive a "service-tax burden ratio," per capita expenditures (total and by specific function) were divided by total tax burden. Of particular interest were the differences by sex and household-status in the efficiency of poverty-related services. If greater benefit, as shown by tax efficiency figures, is derived by women, then any inequities created by a regressive tax structure would be at least partially alleviated.

PATTERNS OF PER CAPITA PERSONAL INCOME

The fact that women generally earn significantly lower wages than men has been well-documented. The report of the Twentieth Century Fund Task Force on Women and Employment indicates that (1) working women earn, on the average, only 58% of what working men earn; (2) women who want to work are much more likely than men to be employed; (3) most women work in "female occupations" (stenographers, teachers, waitresses, household workers), which are often neither unionized nor protected by strong federal legislation; (4) more than one-third of the families headed by women live in poverty, compared with only about 12% of all families; and (5) women's chances for top management jobs are slim, regardless of their abilities.[4]

What has not been well-documented is the *extent* of income inequality between males and females, particularly within the various household groups. The reason for this lack of data is the failure of the U. S. Census Bureau to report per capita income figures by household-status or by sex for Standard Metropolitan Statistical Areas. To obtain these per capita personal income figures, it was necessary to make extensive calculations. Per capita income was computed by taking the median (in terms of dollars) for each of the eleven categories of income, then multiplying the median figures by the total number of persons in each income category, adding the total income earned by each household-status group, and dividing this total earned income by the total number of persons in each household-status group. Consequently, even these per capita income figures were approximations (though it can be argued they are close approximations) of the actual per capita incomes of these various household-status groups. An intentional choice was made to analyze only *employed* persons since they bear the tax burdens, whereas unemployed persons do not.

The figures in Table 1 indicate that a strong relationship exists between sex and per capita income, or, in other words, between sex and income equality. Within the total population, males have higher per capita incomes than do females. Specifically, male heads of household have per capita incomes twice those of female heads of household. The disparity in per capita incomes for single males and females is somewhat less, single male per capita incomes being, on the average, one and one-half times greater than those of single female wage earners. The explanation for this, of course, is directly related to

TABLE 1. *Per Capita Income of Employed Persons Living in SMSA's Over 250,000, By Household-Status Group*

Household-Status	Per Capita Income (Ranked from Highest to Lowest)[a]	Percent Difference in Income[b]
Male heads of household	$8,526	—
Males—primary (single)	5,796	-32%
Female heads of household	4,407	-48
Females—primary (single)	3,892	-54
Females—wives of heads	3,307	-61

Source: Calculated from *Census of Population, 1970,* Table 194.

[a]Per capita income is computed by taking the median (in terms of dollars) for each of the eleven categories of income, then multiplying the median figures by the total number of persons in each income category, adding the total income earned by each household-status group, and dividing this total earned income by the total number of persons in each household-status group.

[b]Percent difference in income figures are based on the per capita personal incomes of male heads of household.

the type of employment of each group. It has been well-established that differential employment is the basis of economic sex discrimination.

The results in Table 1 indicate that per capita income is related not only to sex, but also to household-status within each gender group. Both male and female heads of household have higher per capita incomes than single (primary) individuals. The explanation for this lies in the median age of the different groups: single individuals are no doubt younger than heads of household, less experienced in the labor market, and more subject to periodic unemployment and temporary layoffs.

The most surprising result of the comparison of per capita incomes was that female heads of household were found to have a higher per capita income than other female household-status groups. Much of the previous research on the economic plight of women has indicated that families headed by women are much more apt to be poverty-stricken than other families.[5] The seeming inconsistency here probably results from the fact that poverty levels are calculated by taking into consideration not only income, but also the number of family members. Per capita income, on the other hand, reflects only the average income earned by a certain group, not the number of people who are being supported by the income. Therefore, although female heads of household have a higher per capita income as a group than wives of heads or primary (single) females, they are in reality relatively poorer due to the number of persons that income must support. Also to be considered is the fact that need undoubtedly is an incentive to seek higher-paying jobs. Although the income of wives of heads (married females) may be critical to the family's overall standard of living, it may not be as critical for meeting basic needs. Wives may not be as willing to make the same sacrifices (irregular shifts, overtime, etc.) as female heads of household in order to earn higher salaries. It stands to reason that any person in the situation where there are two wage earners, as opposed to one, has much more flexibility in choosing conditions of employ-ment.[6] Another contributing factor to the relatively low incomes of working wives is that married women face certain stereotypes in the labor market: "they won't last," "they aren't reliable," "they quit," "they get pregnant," and they have child care responsibilities that take them from the job an inordinate amount of time.

In summary, the results of the comparison of means analysis of per capita personal incomes by household-status group and sex showed that income inequalities do exist between males and females and between different house-hold-status groups. These findings are evidence that a linkage exists between income inequalities, sex, and household-status.

GENERAL TAX BURDEN PATTERNS

By Household Status. Tax burdens were defined in terms of the relation-ship between per capita tax revenue and per capita personal income. By defi-nition, then, the focus was on the *equity* of the tax structure, or the relation-ship between the taxes paid and the ability of certain groups to pay. The anal-ysis focused not only on the total tax burden, but on each of its components as well — the property tax burden and the nonproperty tax burden.

The property tax has long been recognized as the most regressive of all local government taxes. A property tax is a "government levy on certain phys-ical or tangible assets that are claims to future services."[7] While the common tendency is to characterize the local government property tax as a tax on homeowners, it is important to recognize that non homeowners also bear a property tax burden as a result of landlords "shifting forward" property taxes in the form of rents charged. Since poorer people spend greater percentages of their incomes for housing than well-to-do persons, property taxes are much more burdensome for the poor than for the rich. That is, they are highly re-gressive taxes.

The two most commonly used nonproperty taxes at the local level are the income tax and the sales tax — both regressive taxes. Sales taxes take larger shares of the incomes of poor people, who must spend most of their incomes buying basic necessities that are subject to tax. Income taxes at the local level, unlike those at the state or national level, tend to take fixed proportions of personal incomes, typically one percent.[8]

It is appropriate at this point to comment on the limitations of the data. It is impossible to disaggregate taxes paid by each household-status group and each gender group from total taxes collected from all persons within an SMSA. By necessity, tax burden must be calculated by dividing per capita tax revenue for all residents of an SMSA by the per capita personal income figures for each of the designated control groups. This discrepancy between actual taxes paid by each group and the per capita tax revenue figures that are, by necessity, used in the tax burden calculations can be somewhat compensated for by taking into account the highly regressive nature of local government tax structures (property and nonproperty). These figures, imperfect as they are, aid in determining whether linkages exist between tax burdens, house-hold-status, and sex. If these linkages are found to exist, it will confirm one of the earlier hypotheses, namely that local government tax structures are in-equitable. That is, local tax structures place undue stress on the finances of those least able to bear the strain.

The figures in Table 2 support earlier hypotheses suggesting linkages be-tween tax burdens (total, property, and nonproperty), household-status, and gender. Examining first the linkage between tax burdens and household-status, it was found that heads of household generally bear a much lighter tax burden than do single (primary) individuals. This is, of course, related to the differences in income levels of heads of household as compared with single persons. The results of the previous comparison of per capita personal income by household-status showed that a perfect inverse relationship exists between per capita income and tax burdens.

The linkage between tax burdens and gender was also clear (see Table 2). The disparity between tax burdens borne by each household-status group is less for females than for males. This can be explained by the tendency of female incomes not to vary greatly, regardless of household-status. A word of caution must be expressed regarding comparison of the tax burdens of males and females, particularly those of male and female heads of household. As previously stated, the two groups were not comparable; male heads of house-hold may have their tax burdens lightened by the presence of a working wife, whereas female heads of household must bear the entire tax burden for them-selves and their dependents. By definition, these dependents do not include an adult male residing in the home. Since the two head of household groups were not comparable, the result is a false inflation of the tax burden borne by wives of heads of household. The effect of combining the incomes of male heads of household and their working wives would be to generally deflate the high tax burdens of working wives, while somewhat inflating the burdens of male heads of household. However, the disparity between tax burdens borne by male and female heads of household still exists as a result of the regressive nature of local government tax structures and the differences in per capita personal incomes. In fact, female heads of household having no male with whom to "share the tax burden" bear a much heavier tax burden than either married or single males.

The only truly comparable tax burden figures were those of single males and females, both self-supporting. When a comparison was made of the total tax burdens borne by each of these groups, it was observed that tax burdens borne by single females are one and one-half times heavier than those borne by single males. Even if the weaknesses of the data (the difference between actual taxes paid and per capita taxes) were eliminated, it would not diminish the linkage between tax burdens and gender due to the differences in per capita income and the regressiveness of local tax structures.

By Region. The figures shown in Table 3 indicate that when a control is made for region (as a surrogate measure of cost-of-living differences among SMSA's), the relationships between tax burdens (total, property, and non-

TABLE 2. Tax Burdens of Employed Persons Living in SMSA's Over 250,000, By Household-Status Group

Household-Status	Total Tax Burden[a]	Increase in Total Tax Burden[b]	Property Tax Burden	Increase in Property Tax Burden	Nonproperty Tax Burden	Increase in Nonproperty Tax Burden
Male heads of household	3.0%	—	2.5%	—	.5%	—
Males—primary (single)	4.0	+33.0%	3.4	+36.0%	.6	+20.0%
Female heads of household	5.4	+56.0	4.5	+84.0	.9	+80.0
Females—primary (single)	6.0	+100.0	5.1	+104.0	1.0	+100.0
Females—wives of heads	7.0	+133.0	6.0	+140.0	1.1	+120.0

Source: Calculated from "'Local Government in Metropolitan Areas,'' vol. 5, Table 12, Census of Governments, 1972.
[a]Tax burden is the relationship between per capita tax revenue and per capita personal income. Tax burden is calculated by dividing per capita tax revenues by per capita personal income (per capita tax revenue/per capita personal income).
[b]Increase-in-tax-burden figures are based on the tax burden of male heads of household.

TABLE 3. Tax Burdens of Employed Persons Living in SMSA's Over 250,000, By Region and Household-Status Group

Household-Status	Total Tax Burden[a] Region[b]				Property Tax Burden Region				Nonproperty Tax Burden Region			
	NE	S	NC	W	NE	S	NC	W	NE	S	NC	W
Male heads of household	4.3%	2.2%	2.7%	3.2%	3.4%	1.7%	2.5%	2.8%	.9%	.5%	.3%	.5%
Males—primary (single)	4.5	3.2	4.2	4.8	3.8	2.4	3.8	4.1	.7	.8	.4	.7
Female heads of household	6.0	4.6	5.5	6.0	5.2	3.5	5.1	5.2	.9	1.1	.6	.9
Females—primary (single)	6.7	4.8	6.4	6.8	5.7	3.6	5.9	5.8	1.0	1.1	.7	1.0
Females—wives of heads	7.9	5.3	7.7	8.3	6.8	4.1	7.0	7.1	1.2	1.3	.8	1.2
All males	4.9	3.5	4.7	4.9	4.2	2.7	4.2	4.1	.8	.8	.7	.7
All females	7.8	6.0	7.2	8.1	6.8	4.6	6.5	6.9	1.3	1.4	.9	1.2

Source: Calculated from "'Local Government in Metropolitan Areas'', vol. 5, Table 12, Census of Governments, 1972.
[a]Tax burden is the relationship between per capita tax revenue and per capita personal income. Tax burden is calculated by dividing per capita tax revenue by per capita personal income (per capita tax revenue/per capita personal income).
[b]The regional classification is NE = Northeast; S = South; NC = North Central (Midwest); and W = West.

property), household-status, and sex still exist. Tax burdens were generally found to be heaviest for all persons (regardless of household-status or sex) who live in Northeastern SMSA's and lightest for persons living in Southern SMSA's. This finding will become even more important in the subsequent analysis of tax efficiencies.

By Population Size. The figures shown in Table 4 indicate that when a control is made for differences in population size (to compensate for differences in economies of scale and in number of services provided), the relationships between tax burdens of all types, household-status, and sex are still observable. Generally, tax burdens are heaviest for all persons living in the largest metropolitan areas (over one million). Previous research has indicated that tax burdens are generally heavier in larger metropolitan areas than in smaller metropolitan areas due to the provision of a wider range of services and a greater expectation of and need for provisions of poverty-related services, such as welfare, health, hospitals, and housing and urban renewal. This is another point to be reemphasized in the analysis of local government tax efficiency.[9]

In summary, even as "crude" as the figures may be, they do demonstrate that local government tax structures are, because of their regressiveness, inequitable. This inequity affects females more than males, and single persons more than married persons. These findings may be interpreted as evidence of the bias of local government officials who write tax laws, which reflect a society that stresses the values of a family structure headed by males.

TAX EFFICIENCY PATTERNS

Tax efficiency was defined in terms of the relationship between the services an individual or household receives from the expenditures of the government and the tax burdens he or she bears as a result of the government's taxation policies. This was also referred to as the "service-tax burden ratio."[10] To date, the best available measures of the benefits an individual receives from the expenditures of his or her local government is per capita expenditures both for total services provided and for specific services provided.

An examination was made of not only the general tax efficiency for all services, but also of the efficiency of the tax structure in providing for the so-called poverty-linked services (welfare, health, hospitals, and housing and urban renewal). If greater benefit, as shown by tax efficiency figures, is received by those most in need of aid, the inequities created by a highly regressive local government structure would be at least partially alleviated. If a linkage is found between tax inefficiency, household-status, and gender, it would demonstrate the "costs" of inequitable tax structures, for those persons most unfairly taxed in relation to their ability to pay place a greater stress than others on the system by demanding and requiring increased governmental services, usually the poverty-linked services. Even more basic, it would demonstrate the "costs" of poorer, often unequal, pay for employed women for the entire economic and governmental system.

TABLE 4. Tax Burden of Employed Persons Living in SMSA's Over 250,000, By Population Size and Household-Status Group

Household-Status	Total Tax Burden[a]			Property Tax Burden			Nonproperty Tax Burden		
	Population Size			Population Size			Population Size		
	1,000,000 and over	500,000-999,999	250,000-499,999	1,000,000 and over	500,000-999,999	250,000-499,999	1,000,000 and over	500,000-999,999	250,000-499,999
Male heads of household	3.4%	2.8%	3.5%	2.9%	2.2%	2.8%	.5%	.5%	.7%
Males—primary (single)	4.7	4.1	3.8	4.1	3.3	3.2	.8	.8	.6
Female heads of household	6.5	5.5	5.2	5.7	4.4	4.4	1.0	1.1	.8
Females—primary (single)	7.0	6.0	5.8	6.1	4.8	4.9	1.1	1.2	.9
Females—wives of heads	8.7	7.1	6.9	7.6	5.8	5.8	1.4	1.4	1.0
All males	5.4	4.1	4.0	4.6	3.2	3.3	1.0	.8	.7
All females	8.1	7.0	6.8	7.1	5.6	5.6	1.4	1.5	1.1

Source: Calculated from "Local Government in Metropolitan Areas," vol. 5, Table 12, Census of Governments, 1972.
[a]Tax burden is the relationship between per capita tax revenue and per capita personal income (per capita tax revenue/per capita personal income).

Again, it is necessary to comment on the imperfections of the data. First, it was impossible to disaggregate the service level figures. No precise determination could be made of how much is spent per capita on each household-status or gender group. Consequently, service level measures were for the entire population. One consolation was that certain groups receive more of certain types of services than other groups. Thus, by comparing the general efficiency of the tax structure for all services, it was possible to get a general "feel" for the overall efficiency of local government tax structures.

General Tax Efficiency (All Services). The figures in Table 5 indicate that the efficiency of local government tax structures is indeed related to household-status and sex. When a specific focus is made on the tax efficiency of all services provided by the local governments, it is found that males receive greater returns on their tax dollars through services than females. When analyzed by household-status group, it was found that heads of household receive the most in return for taxes paid. However, these figures may be somewhat misleading since their proportion of services received is diminished by the number of dependents who must share the proportion of services received for the entire household. But even so, female heads of household get less in return for taxes paid than male heads of household, many of whom are further aided by working wives. These results seem to indicate that local government tax structures are not only inequitable, but also inefficient in delivering services to those most in need of the services within their populations.

Table 5 also indicates that the relationships between tax efficiency, household-status, and sex hold when region and population, respectively, are held constant. Tax structures are most inefficient for all persons, regardless of group, living in the Northeastern SMSA's and most efficient for persons living in Southern SMSA's. Much of this can be explained by the eroding tax base of northern SMSA's, coupled with the necessity of providing a greater number of services as a result of tradition.

Tax Efficiency: Poverty-Related Services. If it is assumed, as it was by Netzer, that services received are progressive related to income, then one would expect to find that local government tax structures are efficient in the provision of poverty-related services—i.e., they are delivered to those in the greatest need.[11] Again, a note of caution must be made regarding the disaggregation of service level figures. However, as Table 6 indicates, the tax structures of these 125 SMSA's over 250,000 population are *inefficient* in their provision of welfare, hospitals, health, and housing and urban renewal services, particularly to females. It might properly be argued that female heads of household receive greater proportions of the funds spent on these services, especially health and welfare services, than male heads of household. But it might also be argued that hospitals and housing and urban renewal services would be equally likely to benefit males and females, though it can be observed that these services also are inefficiently provided for by the tax structures of metropolitan governments.

In summary, local government tax structures, in addition to being inequitable, are also inefficient. The effects of these weaknesses of local tax

TABLE 5. General Tax Efficiency (All Services) for Employed Persons Living in SMSA's Over 250,000, By Region, Population Size and Household-Status Group

Household-Status	General Tax Efficiency[a]	Region[b]				Population Size		
		NE	S	NC	W	1,000,000 and over	500,000- 999,999	250,000- 499,999
Male heads of household	18.874	17.790	19.694	18.463	19.315	18.349	19.489	17.948
Males—primary (single)	12.809	12.167	13.570	12.210	13.057	12.966	13.267	12.544
Female heads of household	9.670	9.121	9.382	10.067	10.313	10.773	9.829	9.197
Females—primary (single)	8.602	8.137	9.035	7.950	9.234	8.807	9.034	8.330
Females—wives of heads	7.359	6.897	8.127	6.637	7.540	7.104	7.610	7.084
All males	11.416	10.405	13.192	11.027	10.108	13.283	12.934	11.161
All females	6.361	5.769	7.315	6.150	5.718	7.972	7.166	6.098

[a]Tax efficiency (the service-tax burden ratio) is the relationship between the benefits an individual or household receives from the government's expenditure policies and the tax burden he/she bears as a result of the government's taxation policies. General tax efficiency is calculated by dividing total per capita expenditures for all services (highways, health, fire, police, sewerage, sanitation, parks and recreation, housing and urban renewal, and libraries) by total tax burden (per capita expenditures/total tax burden). The larger the figure, the more efficient is the return on the tax dollar.

[b]The regional classification is: NE = Northeast; S = South; NC = North Central (Midwest); and W = West.

TABLE 6. Tax Efficiency (Poverty-Related Services) for Employed
Persons Living in SMSA's Over 250,000, By Household-Status Group

	Tax Efficiency			
Household-Status	Welfare	Hospitals	Health	Housing and Urban Renewal
Male heads of household	1.066	.858	.231	.577
Males—primary (single)	.718	.582	.156	.394
Female heads of household	.539	.433	.118	.290
Females—primary (single)	.491	.390	.106	.264
Females—wives of heads	.413	.343	.090	.229

Note: Tax efficiency (the service-tax burden ratio) is the relationship between the benefits an individual or household receives from the government's expenditure policies and the tax burden he/she bears as a result of the government's taxation policies. Tax efficiency for each of the poverty-related services (welfare, hospitals, health, housing and urban renewal) is calculated by dividing the per capita expenditures for each service by the total tax burden (per capita expenditure for each service/total tax burden). The larger the figure, the more efficient is the return on the tax dollar.

structures have the greatest impact on females and single persons. Thus, it is possible to observe that a linkage exists between tax efficiency, household-status, and gender.

CONCLUSION

The results of this study indicate that linkages exist between per capita personal income, local government tax burdens, tax efficiencies, household-status, and gender. The existence of these linkages suggests that the economically disadvantaged position of women, especially in the large metropolitan areas of the U. S., affects local government tax structures and, conversely, that local government tax structures affect the economic positions of women. Local government tax structures were found to be both inequitable and inefficient.

The data indicate that males, averaging higher per capita incomes than females, have lighter tax burdens and benefit from greater tax efficiencies. In other words, men, who have higher average earnings, pay a lower proportion of those earnings to local taxes and, at the same time, receive greater benefits for their tax dollars than do women. Specifically, women are consistently more economically disadvantaged than men. Not only are they handicapped within the society by lower per capita incomes, but they are additionally penalized by heavier local tax burdens and lower returns on their tax dollars. Certain household-status groups also bear a heavier brunt of local taxation policies than others. Male and female heads of household have consistently lower tax burdens and benefit from greater tax efficiencies than do single males and females.

In summary, the findings indicate that persons who are most penalized by the inequalities and inefficiencies of local government tax structures are females, low income earners, unmarried persons, and working wives. As Heather Ross, in her recent study of poverty, indicated, "There is nothing in the nature of economic progress which assures that all people will benefit equally. Indeed, one of the important functions of humane government policy is to correct major imbalances that occur when economic activity rewards some people much more than others."[12] If Ross's statement is accepted, it must be concluded that with regard to humanitarianism, local tax policy is in every respect a dismal failure. Rather than helping to alleviate economic imbalances, local government tax policies serve to further aggravate these imbalances. Local tax policy has been largely neglected insofar as its impact on women as a group is concerned. It has been obscured under the guise of neutral impact on males and females. This illusion needs to be stripped away and local tax policy must take its rightful place on the list of economic discriminators.

RECOMMENDATIONS

Alleviation of inefficiencies and inequalities in local government tax structures will occur only to the extent that local officials adopt more progressive (equitable) tax laws and women's incomes become more equitable to those of their male counterparts. Women's incomes will not become more equitable until major changes occur in the employment patterns of women. Specific changes which must be made include:

(1) A broader interpretation of the concept of "equal work." Most businesses and governments tend to have a high degree of sex segregation in their jobs. For instance, clerical positions tend to be "female" jobs, and laboring positions tend to be "male" jobs. "Male-defined" jobs typically pay more than "female-defined" jobs. Enforcement agencies should be encouraged to begin to consider jobs as comparable, or essentially equal, if the skills and experience necessary to perform the job are comparable.

(2) Less sex-role stereotyping of jobs. Breaking down of sex-role stereotypes will take the combined efforts of the Women's Movement, schools, the media, and virtually every other institution in our society.

(3) Greater awareness of sex discrimination on the part of female workers. Enforcement agencies are limited by the willingness of female workers to demand their rights. Traditionally, society has placed less value on female labor than on male labor. Much female labor is still done for no compensation whatsoever. The women's rights movement has done much to raise the consciousness of women to the value of their labor. Many women who strongly reject identification with "women's lib" accept the concept of "equal pay for equal work." However, they are usually thinking of "identical" work. Greater resocialization effort needs to be put into placing a higher value on "women's work."

(4) Greater enforcement effort on the part of federal agencies, such as the Equal Employment Opportunity Commission (EEOC), the Wage and Hour

Division of the Department of Labor, and the Office of Federal Contract Compliance. This, by necessity, means a greater monetary commitment by the federal government to provide the staff necessary for investigation and litigation, but it also implies the willingness of the agencies to withdraw federal funds or cancel contracts when compliance is not forthcoming.

NOTES

1. See the following: U. S. Department of Labor, *Economic Report of the President* (Washington, D. C.: Government Printing Office, 1973); U. S. Department of Labor, Manpower Administration, *Manpower Report of the President* (Washington, D. C.: Government Printing Office, Apr. 1971); U. S. Women's Bureau, *1969 Handbook on Women Workers* (Washington, D. C.: Government Printing Office, 1969); Victor Fuchs, "Differences in Hourly Earnings Between Men and Women," *Monthly Labor Review*, May 1971, pp. 9-15; Barbara Bergmann and Irman Adelman, "The 1973 Report of the Council of Economic Advisors: The Economic Role of Women," *American Economic Review*, vol. 63 (1973), pp. 509-14; Jessie Bernard, *Women and the Public Interest; An Essay on Policy and Protest* (Chicago: Atherton, 1971); Juanita Kreps, *Sex in the Marketplace: American Women at Work* (Baltimore: The Johns Hopkins University Press, 1971); and Twentieth Century Fund Task Force on Women and Employment, *Exploitation From 9 to 5* (Lexington, Mass.: Lexington, 1975).

2. See Alan K. Campbell and Seymour Sacks, *Metropolitan America: Fiscal Patterns and Governmental Systems* (New York: The Free Press, 1967); Seymour Sacks and John Callahan, "Central City-Suburban Disparity," in Advisory Commission on Intergovernmental Relations, *City Financial Emergencies: The Intergovernmental Dimension* (Washington, D. C.: Government Printing Office, July 1973); and Robert B. Pettengill and Jogendar S. Uppall, *Can Cities Survive? The Fiscal Plight of American Cities* (New York: St. Martin's Press, 1974).

3. U. S. Department of Commerce, Bureau of the Census, *Census of Population, 1970* (Washington, D. C.: Government Printing

Office, 1970), Appendix B, p. 23.

4. Twentieth Century Fund Task Force, p. 3.

5. *Economic Report of the President*, p. 108.

6. Jessie Bernard, *The Future of Motherhood* (New York: Dial, 1974), ch. 10.

7. Werner Z. Hirsch, *The Economics of State and Local Government* (New York: McGraw Hill, 1970), p. 25.

8. Robert L. Lineberry and Ira Sharkansky, *Urban Politics and Public Policy* (New York: Harper and Row, 1971), p. 193.

9. Susan A. MacManus, "Tax Burdens of American Cities and Suburbs: A Comparative Analysis," mimeographed, University of Houston, 1976.

10. For discussions of the concept and measurement of tax efficiency, see Charles M. Tiebout, "A Pure Theory of Local Expenditures," *Journal of Political Economy*, vol. 64 (1956), pp. 416-24; Peter Mieszkowski, "The Property Tax: An Excise Tax or a Profits Tax?" *Journal of Public Economics*, vol. 1 (1974), pp. 73-96; Stephen A. Miller and William K. Tabb, "A New Look At a Pure Theory of Local Expenditures," *National Tax Journal*, vol. 26 (1973), pp. 161-76; and Robert L. Lineberry and Robert C. Welch, "Who Gets What: Measuring and Distribution of Urban Public Services," *Social Science Quarterly*, vol. 54 (1974), pp. 700-12.

11. Dick Netzer, *The Economics of the Property Tax* (Washington, D. C.: The Brookings Institution, 1966).

12. Heather Ross, "Poverty: Women and Children Last," in *Economic Independence for Women: The Foundation for Equal Rights*, ed. Jane Roberts (Beverly Hills, Calif.: Sage, 1976), p. 137.

The Future of Women's Studies

As Women's Studies moves into its second decade of existence, continuing change can be expected. The articles in this collection address this history as well as demonstrate recent research applications to Women's Studies. However, courses and research on women, while not brand-new ideas now, still continue to experience dilemmas peculiar to Women's Studies. Some of these issues occur in the areas of program administration, program structure, course content, faculty, research, community and student needs, evaluation, and inter-program organization.

PROGRAM ADMINISTRATION

Some of the earliest efforts in the 1960s developed the concept of Women's Studies as courses on and by women that were to reflect a female- rather than male-originated administration and organization. Various types of collective approaches to Women's Studies then emerged in opposition to hierarchical forms of organization, which were believed to be historically of male-making. The feminist collectives often included not only faculty involved in the teaching of Women's Studies but representatives of student, community, and administration interests, all of whose input was desired in the planning and administering of Women's Studies programs. As Women's Studies has become more widespread, a second administrative type has resulted and now includes programs and departments organized along traditional hierarchical lines, complete with department chairpersons and faculty and/or administratively made decisions regarding courses and program. A third type of program, whether of a collective of traditional form of organization, developed outside of academia, often from necessity when the local academic institutions either would or could not include Women's Studies. These nonaffiliated programs, which are usually women's programs in community-based organizations, have often been quite responsive to the community since courses can occur whenever there is an expressed interest. Women's Studies programs, then, have experienced these as well as other models of administration as a pluralism of approach has occurred. The issue for the future is whether such a mixture of approaches is desirable or whether there should be greater consensus among Women's Studies programs in order to more effectively develop the study of women.

PROGRAM STRUCTURE

Program structure continues its own process of development within Women's Studies. While most programs in the late 1960s had a rather random collection of courses loosely held together by topic, and some programs are still at this level of organization, many programs are now becoming more systematic in their approaches to courses. This has resulted in a proliferation of institutions now offering majors, minors, and graduate degrees in Women's Studies. While these programs are moving toward higher levels of organization in order to legitimize their existence, other programs are beginning to question whether this is needed or appropriate. Some argue that in order to be able to question the male-dominated system and develop new scholarship, one must remain outside the structure of degrees and defined programs in order to maintain a necessary perspective. Others note that degree-granting departmental programs can be terminated at the whim of some administrator, a risk diminished by the looser organization of courses spread out across as many different departments as possible. Additional issues concern whether programs should develop departmental status and have Women's Studies course numbers, with all the advantages of internal control over courses that this brings, or keep all courses with department numbers within the traditional system and have less control over the courses but perhaps a more secure foothold in the academic system. As with program administration, pluralism is now the picture, with each institution developing its own particular approach to structuring its Women's Studies courses. Future issues concern whether this pluralistic development of Women's Studies is to be encouraged or whether Women's Studies programs should develop more common approaches to structuring their programs.

COURSE CONTENT

Compounding the issues involved in administrative and program approaches are the multitude of various different contents possible in the courses themselves. In the early days of Women's Studies and at institutions just beginning to develop Women's Studies, the existence of even one course on women in a department was considered success. Now, with more students desiring courses and some having more background than others, lower- and upper-division courses are emerging. Many Women's Studies programs now reserve some course numbers at the upper-division level for seminars on chosen topics and special independent projects as well as maintain general overview courses with lower-division course numbers. The content, then, of Women's Studies is becoming more diverse and even somewhat sequential as programs grow.

In addition, increasing quantities of published material are becoming available for use in Women's Studies courses, further influencing the types of courses that are being developed and offered. The expansion of available literature and interest in Women's Studies has tended to push it toward an all inclusive approach to anything having to do with women. This has led to a debate in many circles regarding what rightly belongs in Women's Studies. Merely picking a topic on women that will enroll students is not necessarily quality Women's Studies. As Women's Studies matures, the issue of selectivity in developing courses and programs must be resolved. The relative importance of topics, of course, depends on the overall goals of the program, and developing the criteria for selection will no doubt result in differences of opinion. Yet, some guidelines need to be followed for course content and curricular direction, both with individual programs and perhaps among programs as well. At present, there is no one set of courses or contents for Women's Studies programs, and this needs to be reconsidered in the future.

FACULTY

The faculty who teach Women's Studies courses came initially from the existing faculties of academic institutions. Since Women's Studies was a new area of interest, most did not have extensive Women's Studies backgrounds, and they were learning and creating materials as they taught their courses. As the second decade of Women's Studies begins, there is an ever increasing number of competent individuals, both credentialed and noncredentialed, with extensive backgrounds in Women's Studies. Some have developed their expertise through the academic process, others through direct action-oriented involvement in the Women's Movement, and still others through a combination of these activities. As the number of those available to teach and counsel continues to expand, the question increasingly asked is what kind of individual should be teaching Women's Studies. Aside from the credentialing issues, other factors such as the individual's sex, degree of commitment to and involvement in the Women's Movement, and political and sexual orientations are having increased relevance. In all probability, this much more extensive array of qualifications than mainstream academia evaluates will continue to be involved in Women's Studies hirings. Often, Women's Studies programs have one kind of individual in mind and the administration of educational institutions has another, further muddling the issue of who is "qualified" to teach Women's Studies.

As the value and validity of Women's Studies within the institutional framework become established, faculty concern with promotion and tenure will continue. In some institutions, Women's Studies teaching, writing, and research are regarded with the same evaluative criteria as any other department or program, and Women's Studies faculty experience no particular difficulty with promotion or tenuring. However, in many more institutions, Women's Studies involvement has proven to be risky, especially for junior faculty, since scholarship and teaching excellence in Women's Studies may not be regarded as sufficiently "legitimate" to be the basis for institutional advancement. Legal proceedings continue as Women's Studies faculty argue their cases on promotions and tenure, defending the legitimacy of their Women's Studies work. Many Women's Studies faculty are forced to maintain dual sets of credentials, one in Women's Studies and another in some existing discipline, giving attention to work in both in order to survive academically. Over time, these issues affect the kinds of individuals available for Women's Studies teaching and are already affecting Women's Studies programs.

RESEARCH

With the growth of Women's Studies courses, there has been a parallel growth in research centered on women. Like the politics involved in establishing courses, there are equivalently difficult politics involved in locating funds for feminist research. There is ample interest in doing research on topics relating to women by Women's Studies scholars, but locating funding often proves to be much more difficult. Public and private research-funding institutions are just beginning to acknowledge the importance of such research, and competition for funding is keen. Often research proposals are judged by traditional standards, such as by the degrees and publication history of the applicant, which may not apply to Women's Studies faculty who have been hired and are working under different criteria of excellence. With graduate degree programs in Women's Studies also growing, increasing numbers of individuals with research interests in Women's Studies are emerging. The issue for the future is to expand the available pool of research funds available for Women's Studies scholarship to match the increasingly well-trained group of Women's Studies scholars and students who stand by, ready to do the actual research work.

COMMUNITY AND STUDENT NEEDS

Most Women's Studies programs are becoming more attuned to the needs of their students as well as those of the community. Student and community members now are often valued members of Women's Studies committees that plan and oversee Women's Studies programs. In some programs, student and community representatives have an equal share of power in decision-making with faculty. Unfortunately, other programs still exist in relative isolation from student and community input. Programs need to provide courses and services that are meaningful to students and community members, who after all are potential students. This can be done only with regular input from both groups.

Women's Studies exists, in part, to give interpretation and study to the activities and impact of the larger Women's Movement. Without this involvement with community women's activities, programs stand to lose their relevance and community support base. Programs need the ideas of community and student groups in order to function, and if the programs and services are appropriately chosen, the community and students groups will benefit from the program and strengthen its impact over time.

EVALUATION

At the very basis of the entire set of issues involved in Women's Studies is the need for programs to become increasingly self-critical through some process of regular evaluation. Some programs have course evaluations on all of their courses that provide ample opportunity for students to give ideas on existing and new courses. Ongoing ties to the community bring another source of informal evaluation that is valuable and necessary. Women's Studies is an evolving field and as such must study its own successes and failures carefully in order to plan future goals. This may include the planning of a type of extinction for some or all of the Women's Studies courses as other disciplines alter their curricula and the planning for new areas of inquiry as women and society change.

INTER-PROGRAM ORGANIZATION

As Women's Studies programs have grown in the past few years, many have done so on their own, without the help of other programs. In a sense, each had to "reinvent the wheel," since there was no formal way for programs to learn about each other and give mutual assistance. This is changing as inter-program organization is beginning to occur. As of January 1977 there is a National Women's Studies Association (NWSA), which has adopted the Feminist Press's *Women's Studies Newsletter* as its own newsletter. The *Newsletter* maintains current listings of all Women's Studies programs in the country and periodically publishes these in a directory. Most states and/or regions within the country now have Women's Studies organizations, some of which have affiliated with the NWSA, which serves to keep programs in communication with one another. The various existing professional organizations have women's caucuses and sections, some of which concern themselves with Women's Studies and provide much needed opportunities for faculty and students to share and receive critical feedback on their work. Publishers are beginning to respond with special Women's Studies mailings and materials. The issue of program isolation is beginning to be resolved as these organizational links are developed and a Women's Studies organizational structure emerges.

CONCLUSION

While this is not an exhaustive set of issues facing Women's Studies today or in the near future, they do seem to highlight the kinds of discussions and plans that programs are or will be facing. Most of these have been addressed in some form in this collection of essays. As women continue to change and grow, so will their demand for Women's Studies courses and programs. The types of courses and the findings of research will also continue to change in response to the female experience. Women's Studies provides an avenue for women to be both the subject and the object of study, rather than merely being the occasional passing topic of study in traditional scholarship. Just as individual women are developing their individuality, free from cultural stereotypes, and women collectively are developing some sense of common experience and purpose, free from culturally isolating processes, Women's Studies is also facing its own issues concerning identity. Such an identity is similar to but also quite distinct from other academic areas. Since Women's Studies is more than just new subject matter and is often distinguished by its new forms of internal and external organization, it will likely continue to develop its own distinction with innovation and creativity.

As this collection demonstrates, Women's Studies is still a new area of interest. The field is open to newcomers who would like to add their skills and insights into the collective effort. One might be cautioned to approach Women's Studies with some tolerance for differences of approach, at least at this point in time, and with a great deal of patience as participants reevaluate where they have arrived personally and professionally through increased involvement in Women's Studies. As the culture begins to respond to the issues raised by the larger Women's Movement, there will increasingly be much work to be done in the classroom and in research, all of which is related to the impact made thus far by Women's Studies. It is an exciting and dynamic area of study, complete with its own unique controversies and dialogues, and it is accomplishing important work needed for the humanization of academia and society as a whole. Its future is very much open and dependent upon all our contributions.

Bibliographic Guide

One of the major objectives of this volume is the encouragement of research in Women's Studies. As such, it was designed to provide the serious student with an introduction to some of the issues that surround the evolution of Women's Studies and to furnish examples of current research by scholars in the field. While the relative newness of Women's Studies on the academic scene allows considerable latitude to those wishing to expand available knowledge, it has also created difficulties for the researcher. The lack of established mechanisms for reporting advances in Women's Studies scholarship has resulted in an unpatterned dispersal of available information.

As two individuals who have struggled with the problem of identifying available resources in Women's Studies, the editors are well aware of the frustration that may confront budding scholars. To lessen this potential and to assist students in their own research efforts, we have chosen an approach different from that of the customary bibliography. Rather than restate the source material contained in the notes at the end of each article, this bibliographic guide will furnish some semblance of order for those wanting to further their understanding of and/or initiate their own research in Women's Studies.

The reader should be aware that the guide is not meant to be all inclusive. The upsurge of interest in Women's Studies has resulted in a continuously expanding knowledge base. The guide will, however, assist in discovering these new sources.

GENERAL TOOLS

Books, Essays, and Pamphlets

The first two places any researcher should go to are the card catalogue and the reference librarian at the local library. In examining the card catalogue, it must be remembered that in addition to examining the contents under the general headings of Woman, Women, and Women's Studies, specific related issues such as labor force, lesbianism, marriage, and femininity should be checked. Once this initial search has been completed and the reference librarian has been consulted for possible leads, attention should be focused on the available indexes and guides to works in print. Among the most valuable are:

Library of Congress Catalogue. Books: Subjects. Washington, D.C.: Government Printing Office, 1950-Present. Use these volumes just as you do the subject portion of the card catalogue. The same subject headings apply. They include all the books catalogued by the Library of Congress. While your library may not itself own all of these publications, it can normally obtain them through an interlibrary loan.

Public Issues File (PIF). The PIF is a collection of pamphlets and article reprints, covering a wide range of public issues. Included in the file are publications of Women's Liberation groups and pamphlets on subjects relating to women such as birth control, economic status, education, and employment. These are arranged by subject.

Essay and General Literature Index. New York: H. W. Wilson, 1900-Present. A subject index to collections of essays. It gives the title of the essay and the book in which it is published. The same subject headings listed in the PIF will apply here.

Periodicals

With increased attention being focused on Women's Studies, there has been a rapid upswing in the publication of articles dealing with various aspects and issues of this topic. These have appeared in sources ranging from the *Journal of College Student Personnel* to the more technical and science-oriented publications such as *Engineering Education.* Researchers should check the following general guides for available material at an early stage in their study:

Reader's Guide to Periodical Literature. New York: H. W. Wilson, 1900-Present. An author/subject index to articles in magazines of general interest. This is an excellent starting point if the topic has received considerable public attention.

Social Science and Humanities Index. New York: H. W. Wilson, 1907-Present. An author/subject index to articles in scholarly and professional journals in the social sciences and humanities.

Public Affairs Information Service Bulletin (P.A.I.S.). New York: Public Affairs Information Service, 1915-Present. A selective subject index to public affairs articles in approximately one thousand periodicals, books, pamphlets, and government publications. Some university research programs have access to this via computer terminals.

If available, the best starting points for information on articles in print that deal with Women's Studies are:

Women Studies Abstracts. Rush, N. Y.: Women Studies Abstracts, 1972-Present. The first such service devoted entirely to Women Studies. Issued quarterly, it indexes and provides abstracts of articles from approximately two thousand magazines. Some issues also have bibliographic essays on some aspect of Women Studies.

Special Issues of Serials About Women, 1965-1975. Edited by Susan Cardinale. Monticello, Ill. Council of Planning Librarians, 1976.

Recent years have witnessed the expansion of publications devoted specifically to women. Because many libraries may not as yet subscribe to these journals, the publishers' addresses have been included:

Quest; A Feminist Quarterly. P.O. Box 8843, Washington, D.C. 20003.

Psychology of Women Quarterly. Human Sciences Press, 75 Fifth Avenue, New York, N.Y. 10011.

Women's Studies Journal. Contact Laurie Levinger, Languages, Sciences, and Arts, #1058, University of Michigan, Ann Arbor, Mich. 48104.

Journal of the Psychology of Women. Sage Publications, Inc., 275 South Beverly Drive, Beverly Hills, Calif. 90212.

Signs: A Journal of Women in Culture and Society. U. of Chicago Press; contact Editor Catherine R. Stimpson, Department of English, Barnard College, New York, N.Y. 19927.

Sex Roles: A Journal of Research. Plenum Publishing Corp., 227 West 17th Street, New York, N.Y. 10011.

Frontiers: A Journal of Women Studies. c/o Women Studies Program, Hillside Court #104, University of Colorado, Boulder, Colo. 80302.

Feminist Studies. 417 Riverside Drive, New York, N.Y. 10025; or 606 West 116th Street, New York, N.Y. 10027.

The Journal of the International Institute of Women Studies. Contact Barbette Blackington, Managing Editor, Dupont Circle Building, Suite 205-207, 1346 Connecticut Avenue, Washington, D.C. 20036.

Women: A Journal of Liberation. 3028 Greenmount Avenue, Baltimore, Md. 21218.

Newspaper Articles

In addition to providing general information, many newspapers offer more detailed accounts of and perspectives on issues relating to Women's Studies. Because of the historical nature of the evolvement of Women's Studies, the researcher should also check potential information available in the various "underground" newspapers. Aside from general information, many news articles will contain citations and names that will furnish the basis for further data gathering.

The New York Times Index for the Published News. New York: The New York Times, 1851-1906, 1913-Present.

Newsbank Index. Chesterton, Ind.: Arcata Microfilm Corp., 1970-Present. *Newsbank Index* indexes newspaper articles selected from over two hundred United States newspapers. The articles are grouped in thirteen broad subject categories. See the separate guide to these categories to locate the appropriate headings and subheadings. The articles are available on microfiche filed under the categories by year and under the card number within each year.

Newspaper Index. Wooster, Ohio: Bell & Howell, 1970-Present. An index for the *Chicago Tribune,* the *Los Angeles Times,* the *New Orleans Time-Picayune,* and the *Washington Post.*

The Times, London. Index to the Times. London: The Times, 1906-1913, 1914-Present.

The Wall Street Journal Index. New York: Dow Jones and Co., 1957-Present. (Specifically see Denise Daley Balocco, *Wall Street Journal Index 1976: Women's Issues,* Palo Alto, Calif.: Educational Services Bureau of Dow Jones, 1977.)

Index to the Christian Science Monitor. Corvallis, Ore.: H. M. Cropsey, 1959-Present.

Underground Newspapers Microfilm Collection. Wooster, Ohio: Bell & Howell and the Underground Press Syndicate, 1970-Present. A collection of "underground" newspapers on microfilm. Includes many publications of Women's Liberation Movement such as *Everywoman, Off Our Backs, Pedestal,* and *Rising Up Angy.* Coverage began in the mid-1960s.

Government Publications

Among the richest sources of information on almost any topic are the publications of state and federal governments and those of the United Nations. In the field of Women's Studies, the publications of such agencies as Women's Bureau of the U.S. Department of Labor, State Fair Employment Practices Commissions, and state, federal, and U.N. Commissions on the Status of Women are invaluable. In addition, the record of hearings and debates in Congress or the U.N. General Assembly on such issues as the Equal Rights Amendment or the Convention on the Political Rights of Women may be found in the publications of these bodies.

American Statistics Index. Washington, D.C.: Congressional Information Service, 1970-Present. An annual publication that is a comprehensive guide and index to the statistical publications of the United States Government. A tremendously valuable source of statistical information on American women.

CIS/Index. Washington, D.C.: Congressional Information Service, 1970-Present. A monthly service, cumulating annually, in which all U.S. Congressional publications (hearings, documents, reports, etc.) are indexed and abstracted. Includes indexes of subjects and names and bill, report, and document numbers.

Monthly Catalog of United States Government Publications. Washington, D.C.: Government Printing Office, 1895-Present. Congressional documents and departmental publications of the federal government are indexed in this monthly publication. Entries are arranged alphabetically by issuing agency with monthly indexes that cumulate in the December issue. Since the January 1974 issue, it contains three separate alphabetical indexes: author, title, and subject.

Monthly Checklist of State Publications. Washington, D.C.: Government Printing Office, 1910-Present. Arranged alphabetically by state, this tool lists state documents that are in the Library of Congress. An annual index is issued. It also includes publications of regional organizations and associations of state officials in a special section of each issue.

United Nations Documents Index. New York: United Nations, 1950-Present. A monthly annotated list of U.N. publications with subject index. An annual cumulated index is also issued.

In addition, your state may publish a list of printed works issued by its agencies and organizations. This is particularly valuable where the topic has local implications.

WOMEN'S STUDIES AND RESEARCH—GENERAL

Basically research falls into one of two categories. It is person-oriented or issue-oriented. If the student has chosen a person-oriented topic, the following sources will normally generate considerable information:

Biography Index. New York: H. W. Wilson, 1946-Present. A subject index to biographies and biographical articles in books and magazines. Covers about 1,700 periodicals regularly plus collective and individual biographies and autobiographies. Annual with monthly supplements.

Ireland, Norma Olin. **Index to Women of the World from Ancient to Modern Times; Biographies and Portraits.** Westwood, Mass.: Faxon, 2nd ed., 1974. An index to individual biographies of women appearing in 945 collective biographies. International in coverage. Each entry gives birth and death dates and occupation.

James, Edward T., ed. **Notable American Women, 1607-1950.** Cambridge, Mass.: Harvard University Press, 1971. A three-volume set of scholarly articles on individual American women. Each article includes a bibliography. An appendix lists the women included by profession or area of achievement.

Who's Who of American Women. Chicago: Marquis Who's Who, 1958-Present. An annual biographical dictionary of outstanding American women in politics, business, the arts, and the professions.

Biographical data on women may also be found in the standard sources such as *Who's Who in America, American Men and Women of Science, Current Biography* and *Contemporary Authors.*

If one is dealing with an issue or is examining topical possibilities, the following references volumes should provide ample insight into the availability and location of published material. Often these sources will also contain data pertaining to individuals as well:

Boulding, Elise. **Handbook of International Data on Women.** New York: John Wiley and Son, 1976.

Boxer, Marilyn, et al. **Women's Studies Bibliography: Seventy Essential Readings.** San Diego: San Diego State University Women's Studies Faculty, 1975.

Bureau of the Census. A Statistical Portrait of Women in the United States. Washington, D.C.: Government Printing Office, 1976.

Daniels, Arlene Kaplan. **A Survey of Research Concerns on Women's Issues.** Washington, D.C.: Association of American Colleges, 1975. Gives research ideas, resources for going about research and an excellent short bibliography.

Davis, Lenwood G. **The Women in American Society: A Selected Bibliography.** Monticello, Ill.: Council of Planning Librarians, 1975.

Eichler, Margrit. **An Annotated Selected Bibliography of Bibliographies on Women,** 2nd edition. Pittsburgh: Know, Inc., 1976.

Encyclopedia of Women, 18 volumes. Detroit: Publishing Center, Inc., 1975. While this set was due for publication two years ago, it had not been released at the time of this compilation.

Friedman, Barbara, et al., eds. **Women's Work and Women's Studies, 1973-1974: A Bibliography.** Old Westbury, N.Y., The Feminist Press, 1975.

Jacobs, Sue Ellen. **Women in Perspective: A Guide for Cross-Cultural Studies.** Urbana, Ill., University of Illinois Press, 1974. A massive bibliography that is organized by geographic areas of the world and by topics having to do with women.

Lynn, Naomi; Matasar, Ann; and Rosenberg, Marie. **Research Guide in Women's Studies.** Morristown, N.J.: General Learning Press, 1974.

North American Reference Encyclopedia of Women's Liberation. Philadelphia: North American Publishing, 1972. Contains extensive essays on broad topics such as "Women in Politics" and "Women in Education." More useful than these essays is its "Selected and Annotated Directory and Bibliography to Women's Liberation" (pp. 141-182).

O'Connor, Patricia. **Women: A Selected Bibliography.** Springfield, Ohio: Wittenberg University, 1973.

Rosenberg, Marie, and Bergstrom, Leonard. **Women and Society: A Critical Review of Literature with a Selected Annotated Bibliography.** New York: Sage, 1975.

Schlacter, Gail, and Belli, Donna. **The Changing Role of Women in America: A Selected Annotated Bibliography of Reference Sources.** Monticello, Ill.: Council of Planning Librarians, 1975.

U. S. Department of Labor. Employment Standards Administration. Women's Bureau, **Publications of the Women's Bureau.** Washington, D.C.: Government Printing Office, 1972.

U. S. Department of Labor. Employment Standards Administration. Women's Bureau. **American Women at the Crossroads; Directions for the Future: 50th Annual Conference.** Washington, D.C.: Government Printing Office, 1970. Includes a selective list of publications that treat various aspects of the social and economic status of women, primarily with reference to the United States.

White, William, **Reference Encyclopedia of Women's Liberation.** Philadelphia: North American Publishing Co., 1972.

This list is not by any means exhaustive. It does, however, include most of the latest bibliographical works on women or Women's Studies. A careful researcher should also examine earlier publications for relevancy. This may be accomplished through reference to the:

Bibliographic Index. New York: H. W. Wilson, 1937-Present. A subject index to separately published bibliographies and bibliographies included in books and periodicals. Other specialized bibliographies on all subjects relating to Women's Studies may be found here.

WOMEN'S STUDIES AND RESEARCH—SPECIFIC

A number of good bibliographies are beginning to appear that are directed toward specific areas of concern to women. Going directly to these sources will often save considerable time and effort for the researcher. Examples of these, most of which can be found in Wilson's *Bibliographic Index,* are:

Age

Task Force on Older Women, National Organization for Women. **Age is Becoming: An Annotated Bibliography on Women and Aging.** San Francisco: Glide Publications, 1976.

Art

Female Artists Past and Present. Berkeley, Calif.: Women's History Research Center, 1974. Lists women artists, art historians, art teachers, art critics, and other women working in the arts with bibliographic references for some entries.

Education

Ahlum, Carol. **Feminist Resources for Schools and Colleges; A Guide to Curricular Materials.** Old Westbury, N.Y.: The Feminist Press, 1973.

Arlow, Phyllis. **Women in the High School Curriculum: A Review of High School U. S. History and English Literature Texts.** Old Westbury, N.Y.: The Feminist Press, 1975.

Astin, Helen. **Women: A Bibliography on their Education and Careers.** Washington, D.C.: Human Service Press, 1971.

Current Index to Journals in Education. New York: Macmillan, 1969-Present. Overlaps *Education Index* somewhat but provides abstracts for some of the articles indexed.

Education Index. New York: H. W. Wilson, 1929-Present. The major author/subject index to educational material in the English language.

Forschl, Merle. **Women's Studies for Teachers and Administrators. A Packet of Inservice Education Materials.** Old Westbury, N.Y.: Feminist Press, 1975.

Harmon, Linda Anne, comp. **Status of Women in Higher Education: 1963-1972; A Selected Bibliography.** Ames, Iowa: Iowa State University Library, 1972 (Series in bibliography, no. 2).

Howard, Suzanne. **A Selected Bibliography on Sexism and Education.** Washington, D.C.: American Association of University Women, 1975.

————. **Liberating Our Children, Ourselves: A Handbook of Women's Studies Course Materials for Teacher Educators.** Washington, D.C.: American Association of University Women, 1975.

Research in Education. Washington: Government Printing Office, 1966-Present. This monthly catalogue indexes and abstracts the vast amount of materials in the Educational Resources Information Center (ERIC) files. The ERIC file is a microfiche collection of thousands of reports, documents, etc., related to the various topics within the field of education. A *must* for anyone doing serious work on any aspect of education.

Rosenfelt, Deborah S. **Strong Women: An Annotated Bibliography of Literature for the High School Classroom.** Old Westbury, N.Y.: The Feminist Press, 1976.

Tobias, Sheila, comp. **Female Studies.** Pittsburgh: Know, Inc., 1971-Present. A collection of college syllabi and reading lists on Women's Studies including literature, history, social sciences, art, interdisciplinary courses, and cultural criticism. The reading lists are good starting places for research.

Westervelt, Esther Manning. **Women's Higher and Continuing Education: An Annotated Bibliography.** New York: College Entrance Examination Board, 1971.

Geography

Loyd, Bonnie. **Women and Geography: An Annotated Bibliography and Guide to Sources of Information.** Monticello, Ill.: Council of Planning Librarians, 1976.

History

Arthur and Elizabeth Schelsinger Library on the History of Women in America. **The Manuscript Inventories and the Catalogs of Manuscripts, Books and Pictures.** Boston: G. K. Hall, 1973. The catalogue is one of the largest collections of source material on the history of women in America. Lists books, periodicals, personal papers, pamphlets, and nonprint materials.

Goodwater, Leanna. **Women in Antiquity: An Annotated Bibliography.** Metuchen, N.J.: Scarecrow Press, 1975.

Herstory. Berkeley, Calif.: Bell & Howell and the Women's History Library, 1971-Present. Microfilm copies of the periodical collection of the Women's History Library. Includes "underground" newspapers from the Women's Liberation Movement and newsletters from women's civic, religious, and professional organizations all over the world. Coverage of some titles dates back to the late 1950s.

Millstein, Beth, and Boden, Jane, eds. **We the American Women: A Documentary History.** New York: J. S. Ozer, 1977.

Labor and Employment

Astin, Helen S. **Women: A Bibliography on Their Education and Careers.** Washington, D.C.: Human Service Press, 1971.

Bickner, Mei Liang, and Shaughnessey, Marlene. **Women at Work: An Annotated Bibliography, Volume II.** Los Angeles: University of California, 1976. There is also an early volume, 1974, that was singularly authored by Ms. Bickner.

Hughe, Marija. **The Sexual Barrier; Legal and Economic Aspects of Employment.** San Francisco: Published by the author, 1970. *Supplement #1,* 1971. These bibliographies cover the "law and conditions governing employment of women." Limited to English language books, articles, pamphlets, and government documents.

Kane, Roslyn D. **Sex Discrimination in Education: A Study of Employment Practices Affecting Professional Personnel. Volume II: An Annotated Bibliography.** Washington, D.C.: National Center for Education Statistics, 1976.

Nicholas, Suzanne. **Bibliography on Women Workers (1861-1965).** Geneva, Switz.: International Labour Office, 1970. An international bibliography on women in the labor force. Its heaviest coverage is of American, French, and British publications, including government documents.

Phelps, Ann T., et al. **Selected Annotated Bibliography on Women at Work.** Washington, D.C.: National Institute of Education, 1975.

Soltow, Mary Jane, and Wery, Mary K. **American Women and the Labor Movement, 1825-1974: An Annotated Bibliography.** Metuchen, N.J.: Scarecrow Press, 1975.

Woman Executives; A Selected Annotated Bibliography. Washington, D.C.: Business and Professional Women's Foundation, 1970. Summaries of books, pamphlets, reports, articles, and dissertations on women in managerial and administrative positions.

Law and Politics

The resurgence of the Women's Movement in the 1960s and the accompanying rush for equal treatment, particularly in employment, has had considerable political ramifications. There have been a multitude of legal actions and political decisions during this time span that have had considerable impact on women and the Women's Movement. The researcher should be aware of the general legal indexes that are quite valuable in developing information on the evaluation of the legal and political processes with regard to women. Among these are:

BNA Labor Relations Reporter: Fair Employment Practice Cases. Washington, D.C.: Bureau of National Affairs, 1937-Present. Contains decisions in cases under federal, state, and municipal Fair Employment Practice Laws.

BNA Labor Relations Reporter: Fair Employment Practice Manual. Washington, D.C.: Bureau of National Affairs, 1937-Present. "A complete handbook and guide to federal and state regulation of fair employment practices, including full text of statutes and administrative regulations."

Civil Rights Court Digest. New York: Civil Rights Court Digest, 1968-Present. Monthly digest of state and federal court decisions concerning discrimination on the basis of race, creed, religion, sex, etc.

Constitutions, Electoral Laws and Other Legal Instruments Relating to the Political Rights of Women. New York: United Nations, 1968. "Texts of relevant provisions of constitutions, electoral laws, or other legal instruments relating to the right of women to vote and be eligible for election to public office." Covers 129 member nations.

Index to Legal Periodicals. New York: H. W. Wilson, 1908-Present. Offers subject access to legal periodicals published in the United States, Canada, Great Britain, Northern Ireland, Australia, and New Zealand. Includes yearbooks and annual institutes and annual reviews of the work in a given field or on a given topic. Each issue includes a "Table of Cases Commented Upon," which gives the article and reporter citations. Can be used in conjunction with **Women's Rights Reporter** and other legal reference materials. Articles on the Equal Rights Amendment appear here under the heading "Equal Protection."

Index to Periodical Articles Related to Law. Dobbs Ferry, N.Y.: Glanville Publications, 1958-Present. Indexes only material not included in Index to Legal Periodicals. Covers many journals outside the legal profession. Published monthly.

Sex Problems Court Digest. New York: Sex Problems Court Digest, 1970-Present. A monthly digest of state and federal court decisions. Includes cases related to sex discrimination, pregnancy and abortion, sex education, and homosexuality.

Women's Rights Law Reporter. Newark, N.J.: Women's Rights Law Reporter, 1972-Present. A periodical containing articles on women and the law with summaries of recently heard cases arranged in broad subject categories. Also includes bibliographies of recently published articles on the subject of women and the law.

The importance of these areas in the overall framework of Women's Studies is also indicated by the appearance of a number of excellent bibliographical source guides, such as:

Buvinic, Mayra. **Women and World Development: An Annotated Bibliography.** Washington, D.C.: Overseas Development Council, 1976.

Center for the American Woman and Politics. **Women and American Politics. A Selected Bibliography 1965-1974.** New Brunswick, N.J.: Rutgers, 1974.

Krichmar, Albert. **The Women's Rights Movement in the U.S. 1848-1970; A Bibliography and Sourcebook.** Metuchen, N.J.: Scarecrow Press, 1972.

Levenson, Rosaline. **Women in Government and Politics: A Bibliography of American and Foreign Sources.** Monticello, Ill.: Council of Planning Librarians, 1973.

Tinker, Irene, et al., eds. **Women and World Development.** New York: Praeger, 1976.

Women and American Politics: A Selected Bibliography 1965-1974. Eagleton Institute of Politics, Center for the American Woman and Politics, New Brunswick, N.J.: Rutgers, 1974.

Literature

Backscheider, Paula R., and Nussbaum, Felicity A. **An Annotated Bibliography of 20th Century Critical Studies on Women and Literature, 1600-1800.** New York: Garland Publishers, 1977.

Family Life: Literature and Film; An Annotated Bibliography. Minneapolis: Minnesota Council of Family Relations, 1972.

Feminist Press. **Bibliography on Children's Literature and Textbooks.** Old Westbury, N.Y.: The Feminist Press, 1972.

Meyers, Carol F. **Women in Literature: A Criticism of the Seventies.** Metuchen, N.J.: Scarecrow Press, 1976.

Minority Women

Although the following citations apply more directly to black women, many of the same issues face other minority women. The prevalence of source material on black women may reflect their longer participation in the struggle for equal rights. In recent years, however, there has been a concerted effort by Chicanas and other minority women to attain equal standing and recognition both within the Women's Movement and within society as a whole. This does and will continue to have a direct and positive impact on the availability of information on minority women.

The Black Family and the Black Woman; A Bibliography. Bloomington, Ind.: Indiana University, 1972.

Cole, Johnetta B. "Black Women in America; An Annotated Bibliography," in **The Black Scholar,** December 1971, p. 42. A selective list of books and articles related to black women in America including material on African women.

Davis, Lenwood G. **The Black Family in Urban Areas in the United States.** Monticello, Ill.: Council of Planning Librarians, 1973. Includes Bibliography on Black Women.

————. **Black Women in the Cities 1872-1975: A Bibliography of Published Works on the Life and Achievement of Black Women in Cities in the United States.** Monticello, Ill.: Council of Planning Librarians, 1975.

Williams, Ora. **American Black Women in the Arts and Social Sciences; a Bibliographic Survey.** Metuchen, N.J.: Scarecrow Press, 1973.

Psychology

Janovich, Joann, et al. **Women and Psychology.** Cambridge, Mass.: Cambridge Goddard Graduate School for Social Change, 1972.

Psychological Index. Princeton, N.J.: Psychological Review Corp., 1894-1935. An annual bibliography of the literature of psychology and related subjects.

Psychological Abstracts. Lancaster, Penn.: American Psychological Association, 1972-Present, monthly. The most important abstracting service in the field of psychology. Provides summaries of journal articles, pamphlets, and other materials. Author and subject indexes with six-month cumulations. A *Cumulated Subject Index to Psychological Abstracts* covers the years 1927-1960.

Religion

Bass, Dorothy. **American Women in Church and Society 1607-1920; a Bibliography.** New York: Union Theological Seminary, 1973.

Farians, Elizabeth. **Selected Bibliography on Women and Religion: 1965-1972.** Cincinnati: The Compiler, 1973.

Sciences

Davis, Audrey. **Bibliography on Women: With Special Emphasis on their Roles in Science and Society.** New York: Science History Publications, 1974.

Johnson, Carolyn R. **Women in Architecture: An Annotated Bibliography and Guide to Sources of Information.** Monticello, Ill.: Council of Planning Librarians, 1974.

Roysdon, Christy. **Women in Engineering: A Bibliography on their Progress and Prospects.** Monticello, Ill.: Council of Planning Librarians, 1975.

Sex Roles

Astin, Helen; Parelman, Allison; and Fisher, Anne. **Sex Roles: A Research Bibliography.** Rockville, Md.: National Institute of Mental Health, 1975.

Business and Professional Women's Foundation. **A Selected Annotated Bibliography: Sex Role Concepts.** Washington, D.C.: Business and Professional Women's Foundation, 1969.

THE MOVEMENT: ITS LEADERS AND RESOURCES

Barrer, Myra E., ed. **Women's Organizations and Leaders, 1973 Directory.** Washington, D.C.: Today Publications, 1972. "A current and comprehensive directory and guide to more than 8,000 women's organizations and their leaders. Individual women, active in the women's movement through their actions or writings are also listed."

Films by and/or about Women. Berkeley, Calif.: Women's History Research Center, 1972. A director of films arranged by subject. Includes index to film-makers and distributors.

Grimstad, Kirsten, ed. **The New Woman's Survival Catalog.** New York: Planetarium, 1974.

Harrison, Cynthia E. **Women's Movement Media: A Source Guide.** New York: R. R. Bowker and Co., 1975.

Indiana University. **Women's Films: A Critical Guide.** Bloomington, Ind.: Audio-Visual Center, Indiana University, 1975.

Margi, Jean, and Berkowitz, Tanner, eds. **Who's Who and Where in Women's Studies.** Old Westbury, N.Y.: The Feminist Press, 1975.

Peterson, Deena. **A Practical Guide to the Women's Movement.** New York: Women's Action Alliance, 1975.

Resources for Community Change. **Women Behind Bars: An Organizing Tool.** Washington, D.C.: R.C.C., 1975.

Wheeler, Helen Rippier. **Womanhood Media: Current Resources about Women.** Metuchen, N.J.: Scarecrow Press, 1972. A bibliography of multi-media materials about women. Includes books, pamphlets, periodicals, films, multi-media kits, film strips, posters, and music. Also includes a list of Women's Liberation Movement periodicals. A supplement published in 1975 contains additional current resources about women.

The World Who's Who of Women, Vol. 3. Lotowa, N.J.: Rowman and Littlefield, 1976.

Index

About the Contributors

Kathleen O'Connor Blumhagen (co-editor) is an Assistant Professor of Sociology at Pacific Lutheran University in Tacoma, Washington. She formerly was Research Director for the Colorado Commission on the Status of Women, an Assistant Professor of Sociology and Women's Studies Advisor at Colorado Women's College, the Colorado Coordinator for the National Women's Studies Association, and the 1976 WSSA Women's Studies Chairperson.

Walter D. Johnson (co-editor) is an Associate Profesor of Economics and Legislative Studies at Sangamon State University and Head of the Family Studies Section of the Illinois Legislative Studies Center, both in Springfield, Illinois.

Sarah Slavin Schramm is a doctoral candidate in Political Science at The George Washington University. She is the past chairperson of the National Committee to Promote Women's Studies of the National Organization for Women.

Sarah Hoagland is an Assistant Professor of Philosophy at Northeastern Illinois University in Chicago. She was formerly at the University of Nebraska in Lincoln where she chaired the Ad Hoc Committee on Women's Studies.

Ellen Boneparth is an Assistant Professor of Political Science and Coordinator for the Women's Studies Program at San Jose State University.

Mary Stewart is an Assistant Professor of Sociology at the University of Missouri in Kansas City.

Pat Erickson is an Assistant Professor of Sociology at the University of Missouri in Kansas City.

Joyce Griffen is an Assistant Professor in the Center for Integrated Studies at Northern Arizona University in Flagstaff.

Jane Slaughter is an Assistant Professor of History at the University of New Mexico in Albuquerque. She was the Women's Studies Section Chairperson for the 1977 Western Social Science Association's annual meetings.

Sylvia Gonzales is an Assistant Professor of Mexican American Graduate Studies at San Jose State University where she also is Program Advisor for the Robert F.

Kennedy National Hispanic Student Intern Exchange Program. She is the past acting Executive Director for the National Women's Studies Association.

Herbert M. Kritzer is an Assistant Professor of Political Science at the University of Wisconsin in Madison.

Thomas M. Uhlman is an Assistant Professor of Political Science at the University of Missouri in St. Louis.

Laura Katz Olson is an Assistant Professor of Government at Lehigh University in Bethlehem, Pennsylvania.

Susan A. MacManus is an Assistant Professor of Political Science at the University of Houston.

Nikki R. Van Hightower is the Mayor's Affirmative Action Specialist: Women's Advocate for the City of Houston. She was formerly a Visiting Professor in Political Science at the University of Houston.